Reading the Bible
from the Margins

Reading the Bible
from the Margins

Miguel A. De La Torre

ORBIS BOOKS

Maryknoll, New York 10545

Copyright © 2002 by Miguel A. De La Torre

Queries regarding rights and permissions should be addressed to: Orbis Books, P. O. Box 308, Maryknoll, NY 10545-0308.

Published by Orbis Books, Maryknoll, NY 10545-0308
Manufactured in the United States of America

Library of Congress Cataloging-in-Publication Data

De La Torre, Miguel A.
    Reading the Bible from the margins / Miguel A. De La Torre
       p. cm.
    Includes bibliographical references and index.
      ISBN 1-57075-410-1 (pbk.)
    1. Bible—Hermeneutics.   I. Title.
    BS476 .D4 2002
    220.6'01—dc21   2002000619

*To my campus colleagues
who participated in the Fall 2000 "Exotic" debate*

Contents

Preface

This book was forged in the classroom. Upon first coming to Hope College as an assistant professor, I was asked to design a course that would expose a predominantly Euroamerican student body to non-Eurocentric Christian thought. This was not an easy task, and at times the very nature of the subject matter created tension, if not conflict, within the campus community. Nevertheless, my colleagues in the Religion Department totally supported and encouraged me, even when some of them disagreed with my perspectives. Their commitment to intellectual freedom is greatly appreciated. Furthermore, they provided advice and important feedback on sections of this work, and for that I am also in their debt.

One of the courses I developed was titled "Reading the Bible from the Margins." The objective of the course was to read the biblical text through the eyes of non-Euroamericans, in hopes of discovering how the Bible is incorporated by the disenfranchised seeking to foster liberation from oppressive social structures that foster racism, sexism, and classism. Additionally, the course contested how Euroamerican students traditionally read the biblical text, challenging their interpretations constructed within their culture. Many began to read and understand the Bible from the perspective of other groups, with new eyes that inform, strengthen, and complete their faith. If it wasn't for the students who took this course, this book would not exist. On the basis of that experience, I attempted to answer the questions and objections these students raised in the classroom. Any success this book might have is due to the lively discussions that occurred during class. For this I offer my sincerest thanks.

I am also grateful to the administration at Hope College, which made a commitment for a more diverse campus, recognizing that there is much to be learned from those who historically represent marginalized groups within our society. The college's faithfulness in soliciting and hearing voices of color, rather than seeking political correctness by simply displaying faces of color, is an encouragement for those who at times grow weary of trying to develop a more just community. This dedication was expressed to me by the administration when it graciously provided a summer writing grant through The Jobe and Julie Morrison Family Faculty Development Fund in combination with The Norman and Ruth Peale Fund. Because of this generosity, the necessary time required to finish the project became available.

I would be remiss if I did not mention the copyediting done by Jonathan Schakel. Additionally, I am grateful to Anthony Guardado of the Van Wyler Library for his assistance in tracking down sources and obtaining specific articles. Furthermore, the assistance given by Susan Perry at Orbis Books during the creation of this book is greatly appreciated. Her constant editing, constructive criticism, and challenging questions made the finished product exceedingly better than the original.

Last, but certainly not least, I wish to express my heartfelt thanks to my family, specifically my wife, Deborah, my son, Vincent, and my daughter, Victoria. They constantly put up with me storming around the house, complaining about having to finish a section by tomorrow. They believed and supported me when I doubted myself. Their constant unconditional love provided the emotional support needed to finish this book. For this, and much more, thank you.

Introduction

All football players are damned! According to the Scriptures, anyone who plays football is cursed by God and will spend eternity in hell. The Bible is very clear about this. According to Deuteronomy: "The pig, because its hoof is divided and it does not chew its cud, is unclean. You shall not eat its flesh, *nor touch its dead skin*" (14:8).[1] So anyone who touches a "pigskin," another name for a football, is cursed. During my adolescent years, I did not participate in high school football. In fact, most of the team members were bullies who would ambush and beat me up. So I was pleased to find that the Bible provides the justification for their condemnation. Even God forbids the throwing around of the "pigskin," and who am I to question God's commands? All I'm called to do is obey God's word and proclaim God's displeasure with this barbaric sport.

Even though you, along with the vast majority of Christendom, may question my reading of this biblical text, it is a tenable interpretation. All biblical interpretations are valid to the one who is doing the interpreting. Yet my understanding of Deuteronomy 14:8, regardless of how legitimate and logical it may be to me, is still rejected by the majority of Christians. Why? Because my interpretation of this text attempted to justify my bias toward a group of people whom I loathed, football players. Through my interpretation I justified my hatred toward them, and if I am in a position of power within a community, I could use my interpretation to create social structures that would turn my biases into societal norms, justifying and legitimizing the oppression of football players. It is easy to see how I fuse and confuse what I proclaim the Bible says with what the Bible actually states. In my mind, they are the same. My hatred for football becomes the Bible's condemnation of the sport.

Here lies the first major lesson we can learn about reading the Bible. While we may claim that the biblical text is true and authoritative, not all interpretations are true and authoritative. My interpretation of the Deuteronomy passage cannot be confused with what the text actually says, nor with its possible application to our lives today. Yet, we do this all the time. I'm sure you have heard well-meaning Christians make comments like the following: "The Bible says that the woman should submit to the man and take care of the duties of the household," "According to the Bible, God hates homosexuals," or "The Bible clearly calls for a separation of races." In these statements the interpretation of the speaker is given the same validity as the Bible, making the interpreter's words inerrant. I believe in the Bible, but not necessarily in how the Bible is interpreted by humans.

The second lesson we can learn is that we all approach the biblical text from our specific social location. By social location, I refer to cultural experiences which influence a person's identity. Basically, being white in the United States is a vastly different experience from being black or Latino/a. These experiences define the meaning we give to the different symbols that exist in our lives, including whole texts or individual words that operate as a form of linguistic symbol. In other words, we are all born into a society that shapes and forms us. When we turn our attention to the biblical text as the source of our theological perspectives, we participate in a dialogue between the written word and the meanings our community teaches us to give to these words. We interpret the text the way we do because people whom we love and respect— our parents, ministers and priests, friends, neighbors—have taught us from our earliest childhood how to interpret the Bible. While I recognize that exceptions exist, generally speaking, if our family is Catholic, we are Catholics. If they are Baptist, so are we. If they are Pentecostals, we too worship in such a setting. In fact, if we were born in Saudi Arabia to Sunni Muslims, there is an excellent chance we would be bowing our knees to Allah, and if we were born to a Buddhist family in China, we would now be seeking Nirvana. As much as we may want to deny it, our religious beliefs and, if we are Christians, our interpretation of the Bible are mostly formed by our social location, the family we are born into and the community where we are raised.

But what happens when the community that bore and nurtured us has historically maintained biblical interpretations that cause one group to be oppressed? Suppose our local community interprets the Deuteronomy passage about the pig's skin in the same way I did. They might pass local ordinances that forbade the selling of footballs or playing football. They would grow up knowing and agreeing that this is the "devil's game" and refuse to participate. They would even be able to determine who is a Christian and who is a heathen by the person's refusal to touch the pig's skin. How would we, if born into this social location, rise above the interpretations our culture taught us? Even though our oppression of football players would be justified in our minds as being godly, how could we ever be sure we were not confusing the word of humans for the word of God?

All too often we approach the biblical text assuming that it contains only one meaning, specifically the meaning that existed in the mind of God and was revealed to the original person who verbalized this revelation to those who first heard or read the message. The task of the present-day reader of the Bible is to apply linguistic and historical tools to the text in order to arrive at the original meaning, which is submerged in centuries of commentaries and church doctrines. By applying this methodology, the reader believes he or she will be able to ascertain the original universal meaning that remains applicable to all peoples in all times. In the reader's own mind, his or her interpretation, now elevated to truth, is objectively realized, devoid of any social or cultural influences.

But no biblical interpretation is ever developed in a social or cultural vacuum. Most interpretations are autobiographical, where we ascertain the meaning of the text through the telling of our own stories, projecting onto the Bible how we define and interpret the biblical story in light of our own life experiences. Nevertheless, for a textbook on the biblical text (such as this one) to use the author's autobiographical information as a lens by which interpretations are formulated is considered at best inappropriate, at worst unscholarly. Yet, all "official" interpretations reflect the social location of those with authority to make their personal interpretations the acceptable societal norm. Hence, to claim objectivity in biblical interpretations is to mask the subjectivity of the person, groups, or culture doing the interpreting. The interpretation of Scripture can never occur apart from the identity of the one doing the interpreting. Many of us have been taught to read the Bible through the eyes of those in power, specifically through the eyes of white middle- and upper-class males. When the Bible is read from the social location of those whom society privileges, the risk exists that interpretations designed to protect their power and privilege are subconsciously or consciously constructed. Those who are the authority of society impose their views upon the text and confuse what *they* declare the Bible to say with what the text actually states. To counter this, autobiographical interpretations from the margins of society challenge the claim by the dominant culture that its interpretation of the text is objective and thus superior to any other reading.

This is further complicated by those who defend the Bible as literal and true yet have never read the entire book. And if they did, it was only once. Many who argue for the inerrancy of the Scriptures have not seriously read or studied them, except for their favorite sections. In reality, many of them are really arguing for the inerrancy of the interpretations their parents, ministers, or other spiritual mentors taught them. Historically, such interpretations have at times been detrimental to those existing on the underside of society. Although textual interpretations have been used to justify racism, classism, and sexism, can the same text also liberate those who are oppressed because of their race, ethnicity, gender, sexual orientation, or class? To do so, it must be read with the eyes of the disenfranchised. This becomes the third lesson we can learn about how to read the Bible.

Reading the Bible from the margins of society is not an exercise that reveals interesting perspectives on how other cultures read and interpret biblical texts. To read the Bible from the margins is to grasp God in the midst of struggle and oppression. Hence, such a reading attempts to understand why God's people find themselves struggling for survival within a society that appears to be designed to privilege one group of people at the expense of others. The liberation theologian Gustavo Gutiérrez calls this process "a militant reading," one from the perspective of those dwelling on "the underside of history."[2] The Bible becomes more than a text requiring scholarly analysis; rather it becomes a text of hope, a hope in a God whose essence is the liberation of all who are oppressed, all who subsist at the margins of society. Reading the

Bible from the margins, by its very nature, challenges how the dominant culture has historically interpreted the text. When football aficionados read the Deuteronomy text concerning the pig's skin, they interpret the text differently than I do. Their interpretation automatically subverts how I read the text. While their goal is to justify the playing of football, their interpretation also challenges how I read it. It highlights the weaknesses of my interpretation and shows how my social location and biases subconsciously inform and shape my biblical views.

My understanding of how I have erroneously read the "pigskin" passage leads to my own liberation from ignorance. Here lies the fourth lesson we can learn: reading the Bible from the margins liberates not only those who are oppressed but the oppressors as well. When I read the text through the eyes of football players, I am liberated from my own hatreds and biases and thus am able to draw closer to a more valid understanding of God and the Bible, as well as to the football players who are also created in the image of the Deity. Reading the Bible from the margins is as crucial for the salvation of the dominant culture as it is for the liberation of the disenfranchised.

LIBERATING THE BIBLE

Football players aside, the Bible has been used throughout U.S. history to justify the oppression of "people of color" for the benefit of Euroamericans. The genocide of Native Americans, the slavery of Africans, and the pauperization of Latino/as are but a few examples of how biblical interpretation has condoned oppression by the dominant culture. Additionally, the second-class citizenship of women and the brutality experienced by homosexuals have also been justified though biblical texts. As we shall see in future chapters, the Bible has been used to condemn and damn those who were different from the dominant culture. But how? While some may have maliciously forced interpretations so as to enhance their power and privilege, many, including God-fearing Christians, simply accepted oppressive interpretations as truth.

The task of liberating the Bible is difficult when misreading the text has often led to an enhancement of power and privilege. This task is further complicated when those in power believe that tampering with their interpretations is tantamount to tampering with the actual word of God. Yet, if a biblical interpretation leads to the death of a segment of society, we can assume that such a reading is nonbiblical in the sense that it does not describe the will of God. If the message of Christ is one that brings abundant and eternal life, then any message that fosters death is a message from the Antichrist. To read the Bible from the margins is to read from the context of those who suffer death, literally and figuratively, because of the way society is constructed. Those with power and privilege are not cognizant of how their interpretations can foster the oppression of others. Hence, liberating the Bible from these death-imposing interpretations requires a methodical reading of the Scriptures through the eyes of the disenfranchised. In reading the text with marginalized eyes, the reader either claims a disenfranchised identity or commits to hearing the voices of those who are oppressed, diligently looking to the text from within a context of struggles in order to learn God's salvific will.

Allow me to provide an example of what I mean by reading the Bible from the margins. Let us say that we are pastors preparing a Sunday morning sermon. Our text is Exodus 20:8–10: "Remember to keep the Sabbath day holy. Six days you shall labor and do all your work. The seventh day is a Sabbath to Yahweh your God; you shall do no work that day." Most of us, without realizing it, approach the third commandment through the eyes of white middle-class America. This becomes obvious as we prepare the sermon. Every good sermon, of course, has three points, so we must come up with three points, three insights concerning the third commandment. Some might say that (1) obeying the commandment is good for our spiritual life because it carves out a space in our busy schedule to study God's word and to worship with the body of believers and demonstrates our willingness to be obedient; (2) obeying the commandment is good for the health of our family because it carves out a space in our busy schedule to be with them at worship, share a Sunday meal with them, and catch up on what is going on in their lives; and (3) obeying the commandment is good for our physical health because it carves out a space in our busy schedule to allow the body and mind to rest for the grueling week of hard work, it refreshes us so that we do not burn out working like dogs, and it forces us to refocus on the important things in life, such as our relationship with God. While sermons on this passage will vary, the above outline is typical of what we might expect to hear in any given Sunday morning homily. Such a sermon would be soothing balm to the busy and overworked lives of most who are white middle- and upper-class.

Nevertheless, how would this same passage be preached from the underside of the U.S. economic system, read with the eyes of the marginalized? Justo González provides us with an excellent example. He recounts the sermon preached at a church composed mostly of very poor parishioners. The minister began by asking how many within the congregation worked six days last week? Five days? Four days? Few in the congregation were able to raise their hands to any of these questions. Then the preacher asked how many would have wanted to work six days last week but were unable to find employment. Almost every hand went up. To this response, the minister asked, "How, then, are we to obey the law of God that commands that we shall work six days, when we cannot even find work for a single day?"[3]

This interpretation subverts the dominant culture's interpretation, which focuses solely on taking a day off. The poor teach those with middle- and upper-class privilege that God's third commandment is more than the capricious imposition of a Deity to choose one day in seven to do nothing. Rather, God establishes symmetry and balance in the created order. Working six days is counterbalanced with resting one. When we read this text from the position of economic privilege, we assume the privilege of being employed. We are blinded to the reality that segments of our society lack opportunities for gainful employment due to their race, ethnicity, gender, or class. By imposing upon the text our assumptions of class privilege, we are oblivious to the first part of the commandment, "Six days you shall labor."

By listening to the voices of the disenfranchised, we are confronted with our society's failure in keeping this commandment. Our entire economic system is questioned. For our economy to work at top efficiency, an "acceptable" unemployment rate is required. In fact, when the unemployment rate drops too low, the stock market gets jittery and begins a downward turn. Why? Because corporate America needs a reserve army of underskilled and undereducated laborers to keep wages depressed. Full national employment means companies are paying too much to attract and retain employees, which negatively affects their profits. When we consider that those who are unemployed are disproportionately people from the margins, we realize that our economic system is geared to prevent certain segments of our population from keeping God's commandment, "Six days you shall labor." Reading the Bible from the margins, because it is a contextual reading, subverts traditional readings and seriously critiques the dominant culture.

THE BIBLE IN THE REAL WORLD

When the dominant culture makes its reality normative for the rest of the world, the Bible becomes domesticated and hence ceases to be relevant. As long as the United States remained homogeneously white, middle-class Protestant, only one interpretation, theirs, was needed. No other interpretation was considered, especially if it challenged the dominant culture's power or privilege. Such interpretations were dismissed as either erroneous or lacking in scholastic rigor. Notwithstanding, the fact still remains that the United States is undergoing a radical change. If current demographic trends continue, Euroamericans will cease to be in the majority by 2050.[4] This helps explain the recent rash of xenophobic referendums dealing with immigrants, affirmative action, and English-only ordinances.

Unlike previous generations, today's college students will increasingly find themselves in a global marketplace where they are forced to deal with peoples of different tongues and cultures. Even local businesses, seeking to remain competitive, will have larger portions of their revenue dependent on traditionally disenfranchised groups. Churches and denominations will also have to deal with the influx of more diverse congregations. The questions facing these ecclesiastical bodies are: Will they continue to participate in the most "segregated hour of the week"? Will they expect people of color simply to assimilate to how the dominant culture does church? Or will they embrace people on the margins as fellow laborers in Christ with an equal filling of the Spirit of God, which facilitates the reading of the Bible from the margins of society? The continuous unspoken sin of the dominant culture in keeping the church hour white will result in biblical interpretations that remain irrelevant in the real world.

The theologian Karl Barth once said that theology should be done with the Bible in one hand and the newspaper in the other. Today, I would say that the newspaper needs to be replaced with the remote control. Thus, as a good biblical scholar, I turn to MTV as a source for understanding how the world around me is portrayed and the Bible's place in that world. I especially tune into the show titled *The Real World*. *The Real World* is a "reality" show where several young college-age adults from different walks of life are placed together in a mansion, forced to live and deal with each other in an "exotic" U.S. city. Recently, the show's producers chose New Orleans. Of special interest to this book is an exchange that took place between two of the young adults during the ninth episode of the series.

Julie is a religious white woman who approaches the real world from her faith. Melissa is a biracial woman dealing with how the dominant culture sees and perceives her. During their conversation, Julie refers to African Americans as "colored people." Melissa is taken aback by the racial slur and holds Julie accountable for her statement. In self-defense, Julie says that she simply did not know and begins to become emotionally shaken. Through her tears she explains to Melissa how she feels cheated as a result of her sheltered upbringing. Below is the exchange they had:

Julie: I'm learning more in this conversation with you than I did in four years of high school and three years of college. And that's disgusting to me.

Melissa: Damn right! I would be upset too if I discovered, oh my goodness, I know nothing. You're twenty years old, and there are things that are common knowledge—that are common American knowledge—that you have no idea about because wherever you came from or whatever community you grew up in shut that out. But I mean, now that you recognize that, it is your responsibility now to reach out and find that information.

Julie: But I feel like I've been cheated. I feel like I've been withheld from things. It's just not fair! (At this point she breaks down in tears.)

Melissa: You have been, and it isn't fair.[5]

Julie's religious foundation is proven to be ineffective in dealing with real life. The interpretations she believed to be truth are seen for what they are, human perspectives, based on the social location of one group, that utterly collapse when seen from the wider perspective of all humanity. Julie's dilemma is common among young white college students who are seldom exposed to nonwhite groups, except for the negative stereotypes prevalent in the public media. To read the Bible solely from one racial or economic perspective (whether it is white or other) shelters the reader from the liberative Good News of the Scripture. With time, the Bible, or better yet, our interpretation of the Bible, itself becomes inadequate in dealing with the real world.

READING THROUGH OTHERS' EYES

Can I as a Latino speak for African Americans? Or can I speak for Amerindians or Asians? Can I as a heterosexual man speak for women or homosexuals? Can I, who am employed and considered to be middle-class with the cultural capital of higher education, speak for the poor, those who are underskilled and undereducated? No, of course not. Any attempt on my part to speak for other groups, regardless of my noble intentions, would be paternalistic. In fact, I cannot even speak for all Latina/os. For my social location as an exilic Cuban differs greatly from Mexicans, Puerto Ricans, Chicana/os, Salvadoreans, and so on. At most, I can only speak from my social location as a U.S. Hispanic male and hope that this perspective resonates in the souls of other Latino/as.

If I cannot speak for others, how then can I attempt to write a book that explores the biblical interpretations of different groups that have been oppressed in this country? I can do so only by providing a space where they can speak for themselves. While I have no intention of speaking for African Americans, women, the poor, or other Hispanics, I can quote and elaborate on what they are saying and writing. *Reading the Bible from the Margins* will explore how the Bible is read by these historically oppressed groups to liberate those who suffer and those who benefit due to race, class, and gender oppression within the United States.

The primary aim of this book is to expose the reader to a new way of "seeing" biblical texts. Different biblical narratives will be analyzed from the perspective of the underside of normative Christian interpretations to show how the powerless within U.S. society find spiritual empowerment. The specific objectives of this book are thus as follows:

- First, to read the Bible from the perspectives of those suffering from race, class, and gender oppression.
- Second, to investigate biblical protest narratives to reveal models of resistance and struggle against race, class, and gender domination.
- Finally, to examine various biblical interpretations that are used as a source for liberation and for overcoming dominant religious power structures.

Reading the Bible from the Margins will introduce the reader to Christian biblical concepts and interpretations from the perspective of African Americans, Asians, Hispanics, women, women of color, and gays. It is not my intention to try to convince the reader of the validity of scriptural interpretations arising from the depths of oppression. Instead, the book provides persons of the dominant culture with a window into a world with which they are unfamiliar, even when this world is but a few blocks away from where they live! Upon completing this book, Euroamerican readers should understand biblical interpretations outside their social location. Unlike Julie from *The Real World,* the reader will not need to shed tears for being sheltered from how others understand the Deity. Hopefully, this newfound knowledge might assist in the process of race, class, and gender healing as well as foster a more just society where both the oppressed and the oppressor can find their liberation.

Additionally, this book will attempt to liberate the Bible from biblical scholars. While the role played by scholars remains crucial in helping humanity better understand the text, at times we fall into the fallacy of believing that the Bible can only be interpreted by people with Ph.D.'s. Yet the Bible was not written by or for scholars; it was written to and for the body of believers. When we relegate understanding of the text solely to ministers and scholars, the Bible becomes captive to their particular social locations. Most scholars at prestigious institutions or ministers at megachurches are also products of the socioeconomic contexts in which they live. Like all humans, they also read the Bible from a perspective that may not necessarily match the perspectives of those who are not so privileged. Hence, they also read the Bible in such a way that their own power and privilege are protected, many times defending society's status quo. This became obvious during the 1960s when the majority of white churches, renowned white theologians, and well-known white televangelists remained silent during the civil-rights movement. Where were their cries for justice based on the biblical mandate for liberation? In fact, the white liberal churches tried to persuade Martin Luther King, Jr., to slow down the civil-rights movement when he was arrested in Birmingham, to which he made his now famous response, "Justice too long delayed is justice denied."[6] The question this book will attempt to answer is how the faith communities living on the margins of society read and understand the Scriptures and why those marginalized communities can no longer wait to voice their interpretations.

The reader should also be aware that this book is an end product of a course that I teach by the same name. It is a freshman-level course at a school lacking ethnic and racial diversity. In fact, the student body consists mostly of middle- and upper-class white, conservative Christian midwesterners. I am the first Latino most of the students ever encountered who holds a position of authority, rather than what has become for them the norm, migrant or menial workers. When I first designed this course, I faced the challenge of introducing these biblically based students to the Bible. Many of my students begin the course confusing their scriptural interpretations with biblical truth. By the course's end, these same students begin to realize that other interpretations exist, many of which force them to seriously question what they have always accepted as truth.

It is also important to note that for purposes of this book, I will assume that traditions concerning Jesus' life and his sayings have been accurately preserved by the early faith communities. Most biblical scholars discuss the authenticity of particular statements made by Jesus. Did Jesus actually make the statement, or was it added to the text by the faith community? Did Jesus' family actually flee to Egypt, or was this tradition added to reconcile what the faith community understood to be a messianic prophecy by Hosea: "I called my Son out of Egypt" (11:1)? Also, a great deal of scholarly debate revolves around the authorship of several biblical books, specifically the epistles of Paul. Did Paul actually write them, or did one of his disciples pen the letters and place Paul's name on the works?

Analyzing the Scriptures in this manner is beyond the scope of this book. My usage of Scripture is based on how a nonscholar would read the text within her/his community of faith. An assumption is made that the Gospels either contain the actual words of Christ, Jesus' *ipsissima verba,* or the words of his earliest followers, who attributed these phrases to him. Our task is not to uncover the precise words spoken by Jesus but rather to ascertain how the faith community appropriates the text. Likewise, the authorship of Paul's letters seldom becomes a point of debate within the faith community. While such inquiries are important within the academic community, they are less relevant among the faith communities who look toward these epistles for guidance and inspiration. Arguments made in this book for a particular reading will not depend on whether an event or statement is authentic, nor on who is credited for writing a particular epistle. The text itself is accepted as prima-facie evidence.

A final word about my personal relationship with the Bible. I believe in the Bible and approach it with reverence, searching its pages for the grace of God needed to achieve liberating salvation from both individual and societal sins. Yet I do not necessarily hold the same reverence for human interpretations, especially the interpretations that arise from a privileged dominant culture that justifies a status quo that normalizes oppressive race, gender, and class structures. At no time do I question the authority of Scripture; rather, by claiming its authority, this book challenges how the dominant religious culture has forged its interpretations —interpretations that at times mask power structures. By listening to voices that have historically been kept silent in this country and removed from biblical discourse, we can come closer to understanding how the first hearers of the Good News, themselves disenfranchised from the political powers of Rome and the religious powers of Jerusalem, might have understood the words of Jesus.

CHAPTER 1

Learning to Read:
The Importance of Words

When we open the Bible, or any text for that matter, we seldom question how we define the words we find on the printed page. We assume that the words we read, defined by our cultural ethos, have universal meaning within that society. Yet, at a very basic level, words are linguistic signs that point to something other than themselves, something that conveys meaning. Signs as words do not link a name to a thing; rather they link a concept to an image. These signs, constructed by humans, tell us who we are, define others, and reveal how we relate to each other, the overall society, and the Deity. When we read a word, we envision an image, created by society, that is then connected to the linguistic sign. Signs, whether they be words, colors, or objects, represent meanings that go beyond the confines of the sign itself. For example, let's say we are driving down the street and we notice three circles, each with a different color, one circle on top of the other. Say the top circle is red, the middle circle is yellow, and the bottom circle is green. What do you do when you see the red circle lit up? You stop. Society has taught us to stop on "red." What do you do when you see the green circle lit up? You go. What do you do when you see the yellow circle lit up? Do you speed up before it changes to the red circle?

These colors, like words, are signs pointing to an image or concept constructed by society. The red light does not exist to make you ponder redness. The red light has a meaning given to it by society: stop. Yet, the choice of linking the sign "red" with the concept "stop" was an arbitrary choice made by the person with the power to invent the traffic light. There is no intrinsic stop-ness quality to the color red. The first traffic light could easily have used the color purple to mean stop. Regardless, now, as a society, when we see red as a sign, our immediate reaction is to stop, an action we do without much thought. The linkage of the sign "red" with the concept "stop" becomes legitimized in our mind, so that even to suggest to drivers a different concept for red becomes abnormal. Words, like colors, are signs signifying a concept that has become normative within a given society.

DEFINING TERMS

When we do not know the meaning of a word, we turn to the dictionary, which serves as an objective source. We seldom question the dictionary's validity, nor do we challenge how a term is defined by our society. We simply assume the definition given is true and reliable. Yet the dictionary, far from being objective, is in fact subjective. Because words are linguistic signs, the only thing we can expect to learn from the dictionary is the concept that society has historically linked or is presently linking to that particular word. Hence, the definition of the word at times masks the biases of a given society, biases that remain linked to the word as sign.

Let's consider an example by looking up the word "black." According to the *American Heritage Dictionary of the English Language*, the definitions for black include: soiled, as from soot; dirty; evil; wicked; cheerless and depressing; gloomy; being or characterized by morbid or grimly satiric humor; marked by anger or sullenness; attended with disaster; calamitous; deserving of, indicating, or incurring censure or dishonor. The *Webster's New World College Dictionary* provides a few more nuances, specifically: harmful; disgraceful; full of sorrow or suffering; sad; dismal; disastrous; without hope. *Roget's Super Thesaurus* lists a few additional synonyms: diabolical; satanic; nefarious.

Let us now compare these definitions with the word "white." The *American Heritage Dictionary of the English Language* links the word "white" with: unsullied; pure. According to the *Webster's New World College Dictionary*, "white" also means: morally or spiritually pure; spotless; innocent; free from evil intent; harmless; honest; honorable; fair; decent. *Roget's Super Thesaurus* contrasts "white" as the antonym for "black" and defines it as: sunny; bright;

illuminated; cheerful; hopeful; auspicious; favorable; good; angelic; saintly.

In short, our culture has linked the word and color "black" with negative definitions and "white" with positive definitions. This is evident in the old TV westerns where the good guys were distinguished from the bad by the color of their hats. These definitions given to the words "black" and "white" reveal our culture's attitudes toward these colors—attitudes formed within a society that has historically used color to define one's place in the overall community. The lighter the skin pigmentation, the greater the availability of opportunities. By defining "black" and "white" in this fashion, the purity of whiteness and the wickedness of blackness are transferred to the society at large. Rather than confess that the inequalities of society are due to racist social structures, religion (as well as other communal networks) provides the psychological reassurance of legitimacy; in other words, it confirms that the wealth, power, and privilege amassed by the members of the dominant culture are theirs by right. When whites compare their social status with the less privileged space of nonwhites, they fail to merely be content with their success. They desire "the right to their happiness."[1]

In the minds of those within the dominant culture, people on the margins are predominantly poor and disenfranchised not as a direct result of the Euroamericans' privileged space but because of the character flaws of nonwhites, flaws that are reinforced by how the terms "white" and "black" are defined. The plight of the poor, trapped in the ghettos and *barrios* of this wealthy nation, is due to the inferiority associated with their darker skin pigmentation. The victims of poverty are blamed for their own social location; this exonerates the privileged, whose secured social space is dependent upon maintaining a reserve army of undereducated, underskilled laborers. Blackness becomes the color of all that is wrong with America: laziness, poverty, the welfare state, and sin.

Is it any wonder then that when a black man approaches our car, we quickly lock the doors? Or when a black man walks by us, we clutch our purses and hold them closer to our body? After all, by definition a wicked, evil, dirty, satanic man is approaching, and hence our safety and possessions are threatened. Have you noticed that we never refer to a poor person of color as "black trash" because, by definition, using the words "black" and "trash" together is redundant? Yet we refer to poor whites as "white trash" because "white," by definition, is pure and spotless; hence the phrase discloses the internal incongruence of the term. Because the words "black" and "white" as signs are arbitrarily linked to concepts constructed by a society that conveys its biases, we shouldn't be surprised that this particular nation, steeped in racism since its foundation, would link negative connotations to the word "black" and positive connotations to the word "white."

In the spring of 1997, actor Desi Arnaz Giles received numerous death threats for his starring role in a play based on the life of Jesus Christ. *The Passion Play,* focusing on the final days of Christ's earthly life, is performed annually and has historically attracted bus groups from the northern New Jersey region. The controversy began after the first performance, when the audience discovered that Giles was black. As word spread, several of these groups canceled.[2] Why the uproar? If "black" is defined as evil, wicked, and diabolical, it would be blasphemy to define Jesus, who is pure and spotless, as black. Jesus can be no color but white. A portrait of a Christ who is black becomes offensive because it contradicts the definition our culture has assigned, normalized, and legitimized for the word "black."

IMPOSING TWENTY-FIRST-CENTURY MEANINGS ON ANCIENT TEXTS

What happens when we read the biblical text with eyes formed in the twenty-first century? Do we read into the words found in the ancient biblical text the meanings our present culture has taught us? Consider the example found in Numbers 12. The text states the following:

> Miriam and Aaron spoke against Moses because of the Cushite woman whom he had taken for a wife. For he had taken a Cushite woman. They said, "Has Yahweh spoken only to Moses? Has he not also spoken to us?" And Yahweh heard. Now, the man Moses was very meek, more than any man on the face of the earth. . . . And the anger of Yahweh glowed against them, and he left. . . . And behold, Miriam

was leprous, white as snow. And Aaron turned toward Miriam and behold, she was a leper. Aaron said to Moses, "Oh my lord I beg you, do not lay upon us this sin which we foolishly committed and are guilty of." (1–3, 9, 10–11)

The story is about Moses marrying a black woman, placing his family in an awkward situation. The Cushites were a black ethnic group. According to the text, Moses' marriage upset his brother Aaron and his sister Miriam. They were so upset that they chose to confront him. They challenged Moses by saying, "Has God spoken only to Moses? Has he not spoken to us?" All three of them then appeared before God, who was surprisingly upset with Moses' family. The Bible says that God was so mad that he inflicted Miriam with leprosy, turning her skin "white as snow." God punished Miriam by making her white! Note: Why didn't God also punish Aaron for speaking out against Moses? Why is the woman punished and the male spared? Regardless, God relented after her brothers pleaded for mercy.

We read the words found in this story and impose upon those words the meaning our culture has assigned to them, a linkage that includes our twenty-first-century cultural biases. Because racism is so ingrained within U.S. society, we simply assume that Aaron and Miriam were upset because Moses married downward. If a present-day white family member was to marry a person of color, more than likely the family would be concerned about the relationship. Their biases are usually masked by the advice "Think about the children and how they will suffer." We read these biases into the biblical story and conclude that Moses' siblings were upset because a black woman had become part of the family. Yet a closer reading of the text reveals that it was not Moses who married downward.

We first need to ask which people were politically superior in the region. The answer, Africans (specifically Egyptians). African blacks were the ones in positions of power during Moses' lifetime. Hence, to marry a black person was to marry upward. The concern Aaron and Miriam expressed was that because Moses married upward, he might "put on airs." This is why they ask if he thinks that God can only talk to him. This also explains why the text reassures the reader that "Moses was very meek, more than any man on the face of the earth" (v. 3).

Yet race may not be the reason why Moses was marrying upward. Nowhere in the Bible does it tell us that Moses' skin was white. Why then do we assume it was? At this time in world history, there were no major concentrations of Europeans in this area of the world. The Cushite woman may have been marrying down not because of race but because of the socioeconomic position of the Hebrews, a non-nation of people roaming through a desert. Yet, in spite of these sociohistorical facts, the dominant cultures read the texts from within their particular social location, imposing on the interpretation subconscious biases.

How else have we "colored" the Scriptures? According to the Bible, what color were Adam and Eve? Saul, David, or Solomon? The prophets? Jesus? If the Bible does not tell us their color, why do we think of them and depict them on church walls and books as being white Europeans? One of my students once asked, "Where do blacks come from?" After all, if Adam and Eve were the first two humans, how can we explain the development of the black race? In her mind, Adam and Eve, created in the image of God, had to be white. Regardless of her assumptions, I asked her what God used to create Adam. She replied the soil, a reference to Genesis 2:7, where God forms man out of the ground's soil and then breathes life into him. I asked what color is the richest and most fertile soil. She answered black. I then asked if she had ever heard of white soil. She shook her head no. Why then do we assume Adam was white? If God chose the best soil for God's ultimate creation, wouldn't the skin of that creation resemble the ingredient used? Maybe her question should have been, "Where do whites come from?"

Although the biblical text fails to reveal the color of Adam and Eve, leaving us to assume their skin pigmentation, the Bible does record the presence of Africans. For example, in Genesis 10:8–12, the founder of civilization in Mesopotamia, Nimrod, is called the son of Cush, Cush being the most commonly used term in the biblical text to designate a person's black color. The term "Cush" was the name given by the Egyptians to the people living south of them. The Hebrews picked up this term and used it to refer to the people from the interior regions of Africa. When the Hebrew biblical text was translated into Greek (the Septuagint), the most frequent translation for "Cush" was "Aithiops," which literally meant "burnt-face." Although "Aithiops" is translated into the English word "Ethiopian" (not to be confused with modern-day Ethiopia), the term was also used to refer to Africans of dark skin pigmentation with African physical features (wide nose, hair texture, and so on).

In the Hebrew Bible, Cush was also used to refer to the Egyptians. In short, Cush (Ethiopia), Nubia, Put (Phut), and Egypt were not always distinct geographic entities, but can be understood as referring essentially to the ancestors of the same people group, Africans. By defining the terms that reveal the presence of Africans in the Bible, we quickly discover their major contributions. Besides Nimrod and Moses' Cushite wife, we also discover that the prophet Zephaniah is the son of Cushi. The Hebrew word *Phinehas,* a derivative from the Egyptian word *Pa-Neshsi,* means "Nubian" or "Negro." Phinehas is also the proper name of Aaron's grandson (Moses' grandnephew), the high priest Eli's son (during the prophet Samuel's youth), and numerous Jews in postexilic times. Why call a child Negro if he or she was not black? Other biblical characters who most certainly were African were Hagar, Abraham's maid-wife (Gen. 16), Jeremiah's benefactor Ebedmelech (Jer. 38–39), Tirhakah the Ethiopian king (Isa. 37:9), the Queen of Sheba (1 Kings 10), Simon of Cyrene (Matt. 27:32), and the Ethiopian eunuch (Acts 8).[3]

DEFINING RACISM

So far, we have focused on the words "black" and "white." Yet another linguistic sign needs to be defined before we can move forward. This word is "racism," and, like black and white, it also is defined by the dominant culture in order to disavow any personal biases or obligation toward societal racist structures. *Webster's Encyclopedic Dictionary* defines racism as "the *belief* that certain races, especially one's own, are inherently superior to others" (italic mine). Now, most people, when asked if they believe in the supremacy of their own race, would normally answer no. With the exception of white supremacy groups like the Ku Klux Klan, Arian Nation, neo-Nazis, or the Church of the Creator, few people today believe or are willing to admit a belief in their race's superiority. Most would agree, at least publicly, that race does not determine intellectual or any other kind of supremacy. Hence, if no belief of superiority exists, then by definition no racism exists. This is because our society has linked the word "racism" with the concept of expressing a belief. If any traces are to be found, it is either a lingering pre-civil-rights bias or a present day product of ignorance.

For purposes of this book, racism will be defined not solely as a belief but rather as actions committed individually or communally. Most scholars recognize the three united prongs of racism: prejudices (beliefs), power structures, and societal norms. Such a definition asserts that while a person may not hold a *belief* in racial superiority, she or he still contributes to racism by complicity with the present power structures designed to protect power and privilege in certain geographical locations. The mere fact that a Hispanic's skin coloration may be lighter than other Latino/as assures greater success in this country over against Hispanics who display more pronounced Amerindian, African, or Asian features.

For example, during the 1980s, as a young, light-skinned Cuban, I was pulled over by the New Jersey highway patrol and searched because I was a Latino with long hair wearing a bandana and driving a fairly new red sports car. When pulled over, I asked the officer what was wrong. He answered that I was traveling five miles above the speed limit. After checking my driver's license, registration form, and insurance policy, he asked if he could also search my car and my person. Common procedure for speeders? I think not. So I asked why. His response: sport cars driven by Latinos with Dade County license plates were suspected of importing cocaine to New York City. Before racial profiling ever made the headlines, I knew what it meant to be a suspect because I committed the crime of driving a nice car while being Hispanic.

Yet, by the same token, I confess that I need not worry about being pulled over while driving in Dade County. Why? Of all cities in the United States, Miami is the only municipality where first-generation Latin American immigrants have become dominant in city politics. By the 1990s, the majority of city commissioners were exilic Cubans, as was the mayor. The superintendent of Dade County public schools, the state chairs of the Florida Democratic Party, and the local chairs of the county's political parties were exilic Cubans. Also, the presidents of about twenty banks, Florida International University, the Dade County AFL-CIO, the Miami Chamber of Commerce, the Miami Herald Publishing Company, and the Greater Miami Board of Realtors (a post I once held) were exilic Cuban. It is common to find exilic Cubans occupying top administrative posts in City Hall, *The Miami Herald,* and the city's corporate boardrooms. Cubans wield tremendous power in the political, social, economic, and cultural spheres of Miami. Because exilic Cubans surmounted the social structures of oppression, I am the racist or the oppressor when in Miami and the victim of racism or oppression when I leave.

Remember that racism is more than just personal prejudices or biases; it is the product of social structures designed to privilege one group over another. Even though my prejudices and biases remain the same, when in Miami I am the one who benefits from the social structures, hence the racist. Yet when I leave Miami and drive on the New Jersey Turnpike, I am the victim of racism. What changed? Not my biases or prejudices; rather, my social location. Although personal biases or prejudices are not virtues to be emulated, they do not fully constitute racism: social structures do.

This is why, when people of color point out Euroamerica's racism, they are referring to something that goes beyond mere bias or prejudice. White privilege makes all whites racist not because of their possible beliefs of superiority but because they benefit from the present social structures; in the same way, I must confess my racism when in Miami because those structures are designed to benefit me. This does not make all whites evil, wicked people; it simply reveals who benefits in society because of race. It must be remembered that this was not always the case. After all, blond-haired and blue-eyed white Gauls were sold as slaves in the marketplaces of Rome during imperial times, and white Europeans served as slaves to Moorish and Ottoman overlords. Racism depends on which group controls power and uses that power, at the expense of others, to provide privilege for one group. In this country, at this time in world history, the face of racism happens to be white.

In the same way, I must confess that I am a sexist, even though I consider myself a feminist. Because of my gender, I must realize and confess my complicity with sexist social structures, a complicity motivated by personal advantage.[4] When competing with a woman for a job, I hold the advantage of being hired, and at a higher salary, solely because I am male. It does not matter that my personal beliefs are that men and women are and should be treated as equals; the social structures exist to provide me with privilege due to my gender. All things being equal, I prevail over women in the marketplace, in the church community, and in society at large because I am male. I need not hold racist or sexist beliefs; my complicity with social structures protects the privilege that comes with whiteness and maleness.

Racism, as well as sexism, becomes normalized within a society through its customs, language, traditions, myths, regulations, and laws. Those who benefit from racist structures usually do not recognize their existence, making complicity effortless. In fact, racism has become so ingrained in our subconscious that we can actually measure our physical reactions to other races. In a 1998 study conducted at Purdue University, researchers examined the physiological response to an encounter and a physical contact with an unfamiliar person. Fifty-three African American (23 males and 30 females) and fifty-one Euroamerican (23 males and 28 females) undergraduates participated in the study. By measuring facial muscle activity, increased skin conductance, and heart rate acceleration, the study was able to investigate the automatic and expressive effects of an initial greeting and touch from an unfamiliar person. The subjects were met by a female research assistant of the same race who oriented them to the laboratory and attached sensors to them. The research assistant left the room, only to have an unfamiliar interactor enter moments later. The interactor was of the same sex as the subject but varied in racial composition, with half of the subjects encountering a white person and the other half encountering a black person. After a few moments of introducing themselves and checking the equipment, the interactor asked to take the subject's pulse rate.

The results of the experiment showed that when the interactor was of a different race, the subject's heart rate accelerated, skin conductance increased, and facial muscles tightened; in other words, the subject showed internal physical manifestations of stress. These levels were significantly higher when the interactor was a black man (especially among white male subjects).[5] The study seems to indicate that even when we profess to be "color-blind," white bodies physically react when touched by black bodies. Politically correct rhetoric aside, race is deeply ingrained in how we have been taught to see others.

We cannot, however, speak about race as a meaningful criterion within the biological sciences because every reputable biologist understands that race as a scientific category is unsupportable. The human genetic variability between the populations of Africa or Asia or Europe or Latin America is not significantly greater than the differences existing within those ethnic populations. Race is not a scientific notion; it is a sociohistorical concept. Race is not a biological factor differentiating humans; rather, it is a social construction whose function is the oppression of one group of people for the benefit of another. With the exception of skin color and physical difference (hair texture, eye and nose size, and so on), racial character differences do not exist. Rather, race is a sign that signifies who has power and privilege within a given society.

Yet, if race is a social construction, can persons find themselves occupying more than one race? Throughout my life, the Latino/a community where I was raised reinforced the notion that I was "white." Thus, when I gazed into the mirror, I was taught to see a white middle-class Hispanic man. I then left my Latina/o neighborhood in Miami and moved to Louisville, Kentucky, where I eventually took a job teaching Spanish at a local college. I decided to test my students on their ability to pronounce colors in Spanish by pointing at an item and asking the students, ¿Qué color es esto? ("What color is this?"). After pointing to several items throughout the room and soliciting numerous different responses, I realized I had yet to ask a question where the answer would be *Blanco* ("White"). Not finding anything white in the room, I pointed to my skin and asked, "What color is this?" To my surprise, the class in unison responded, *Moreno* ("Brown"). At that moment I realized the dominant culture saw me as brown while I saw myself as white. Regardless of my skin pigmentation, the dominant culture classifies me as nonwhite because I speak Spanish. Without knowing it, I became a "cross-dresser" between two different constructions of race. While in Miami, exilic Cubans as a whole see themselves as being white, not realizing that to the dominant culture we are brown.

THE FACTOR OF LANGUAGE

The 1950s television star Desi Arnaz, best known as Ricky Ricardo in the sitcom *I Love Lucy,* had a sign posted on his dressing door: "English is broken here." This spoken broken English became a unifying source among Hispanics, regardless of national origin. Yet, a presumption exists that all Latino/as are able to speak Spanish. In reality, some speak English, others Spanish, some are bilingual, while still others speak Spanglish. Now, if reading and interpreting the Bible in English becomes complicated because of meanings imposed upon the ancient text that reflect twenty-first-century biases, what happens when we read the text in another language? Those who read the Bible in Spanish discover a text that provides theological interpretations different from those who read the same passages in English. To read the Bible in Spanish is to find different ways of understanding the Scriptures, ways that expand and challenge the normative interpretations of the dominant culture.

For example, the English word "love" usually characterizes how we feel toward diverse objects, persons, and experiences. I love my wife, I love ice cream, I love my children, or I love baseball—these are phrases any one of us would use to describe something or someone who gives us joy. In reality, I do not love baseball with the same intensity or passion as the love I express for my wife. Yet, because we use the same word to describe these different levels of affections, the word "love" loses its intimacy and significance. The Spanish language provides a distinction. *Te amo* ("I love you") is reserved only for spouses or lovers. *Te quiero* (literally, "I want you") is used to connote love toward family and friends. *Me gusta* ("I like it") usually refers to baseball, ice cream, and other things or experiences we like. Which Spanish word do you think is used for the word love when referring to God? The more intimate term, *Te amo*, is used. To read of the love of God is to read about the intimate relationship between lovers.

The English word "you," which can be translated into Spanish as either *tú* or *usted*, also reveals how we understand God when we read the Bible in Spanish. *Usted* is a formal pronoun used when addressing those who occupy a higher station in life. When speaking to my employer, a political or community leader, or my mentor/teacher, I show my respect by addressing them as *usted*. On the other hand, *tú* is an informal pronoun used among equals or for those who occupy lower social standing. Friends, coworkers, children, or employees are usually referred to as *tú*. Which Spanish pronoun do you think is used when referring to God? The informal *tú* is used, not the formal *usted*. By calling God *tú*, God is recognized as one who is in solidarity with the station of life of U.S. Hispanics.[6] God too is from the margins.

A *HAN* READING

When those who are disenfranchised suffer unbearable injustices, they develop an inexpressible feeling in the pit of their stomachs. The Korean community has a name for this pang. They call it *han*.[7] *Han* encompasses the feelings of resentment, helplessness, bitterness, sorrow, and revenge that are felt deep in the victim's guts. *Han* becomes the daily companion of the powerless, the voiceless, the marginalized. *Han*, however, is not restricted to the individual. When social injustices prevail throughout the whole community for several generations without an avenue of release or cleansing, a collective *han* (collective unconsciousness) develops. For many who are Asians, or of Asian descent, life in this country is a *han*-ridden experience. Yet, it is from the *han*-ridden margins that the dominant culture finds its salvation.

The parable of the Good Samaritan is recounted by Jesus in Luke 10:25–37. Jesus is responding to a member of the dominant culture, a promising lawyer, who is asking what he must do to inherit eternal life, salvation. Jesus narrates the story of a man who is on his way to Jericho from Jerusalem. Suddenly, he finds himself in the hands of brigands. Beaten and robbed, he is left for dead. Shortly afterward, a priest who is traveling on the same road sees the wounded man but crosses the street to avoid him. Minutes later, another holy man from the dominant culture, a Levite, comes across the wounded man, but he too crosses the street and avoids him. Eventually, a member from the margins of society, a Samaritan, a person of color, sees the wounded man, has compassion, and ministers to him. He bandages his wounds by pouring oil and wine on them. Then the Samaritan carries the wounded man to a nearby inn and pays out of his pocket for the man to be looked after.

The Samaritan lived a life of *han*. Although the wounded man was a member of the dominant culture responsible for the Samaritan's oppression, the Samaritan was able to take pity because he had *han* inside himself. The ability to recognize *han* initiates a healing where the wounded are able to heal the wounds of others. One who suffers unbearable pain is able to understand and pour refreshing "oil and wine" on the others' wounds. Hence the importance of support groups, where people struggling with the same pain come together to help each other in the healing process. By picking the Samaritan outcast to be the catalyst for healing and salvation, instead of other members of the dominant culture, Jesus calls the *han*-ridden communities located on the margins of society to be the agents of healing for a *han*-ridden world.[8] Those who are suffering *han* should not look to the priest and ministers for help unless they too have experienced *han*.

MULTIPLE CONSCIOUSNESS

If a biblical text can be read and interpreted in several different ways, which interpretation is correct? The challenge faced by those who read the Bible from the margins is that the dominant culture has the power to shape and legitimize the religious discourse. The interpretations of the disenfranchised can easily be dismissed as interesting perspectives that may add some "color" to understanding the Bible, but in the minds of the dominant culture, these interpretations are deemed lacking in scholastic rigor and without any universal relevance. Yet, violence is done to the biblical text when we reduce the interpretations that come from the margins into interesting perspectives among the multitude of possible perspectives, each equal in value and importance. Reading the Bible from the social location of oppression does not call for the treatment of all biblical interpretations as equals, where the interpretation from the margins is but one competing perspective. Rather, an affirmation and an option are made for the interpretations of the disenfranchised, taking priority over the interpretations of those who still benefit from societal structures of oppression.

At first glance, it may appear somewhat arrogant to claim the superiority of one interpretation over another. Why should the interpretations that are formed in the margins of society take precedence over the interpretations voiced by the dominant culture? Is it because the disenfranchised are holier? Smarter? Closer to God? No, of course not. The reason an interpretational privilege exists for the disenfranchised is that such an interpretation is based on a concept known as the hermeneutical privilege of the oppressed.

This term basically means that those who are disenfranchised are in a position to understand the biblical text better because they know what it means to be a marginalized person attempting to survive within a social context designed to benefit others at their expense.

In W. E. B. Du Bois's monumental book, *The Souls of Black Folk,* he introduces the reader to the concept of double consciousness, a concept that describes the experience African Americans endure when they are pressured to forsake their self-consciousness. African Americans (and I would add all marginalized people) are forced to see themselves as the white world sees them. This leads to the disenfranchised defining themselves through the eyes of the dominant culture via common stereotypes imposed upon them.[9] When they begin to read the biblical text, they look toward the dominant culture to set the standards by which the text is normatively read and interpreted. At times, these interpretations are responsible for the maintenance of very oppressive social structures that keep them at the margins of society.

Although Du Bois writes about double consciousness, we can expand his work to include triple consciousness or even quadruple consciousness. If a black woman sees herself through the eyes of a white-dominated and male-dominated world, can her self-definition be understood as triple-consciousness? What if she is a black Latina woman? Does this constitute quadruple consciousness? As a Latino male, I know what it is to be a victim of ethnic discrimination, but as a male, I also know what it means to be the beneficiary of sexist structures. Likewise, because I have a lighter skin pigmentation and lack pronounced African or Amerindian features, I also benefit, to some degree, in a social structure that privileges those closest to the white ideal. I am both victim and victimizer. Our culture's present structures of oppression go beyond a black-white dichotomy. Oppressive social structures are fluid, creating different levels and severities of oppression. Rather than enter into a discussion as to who is more oppressed, it will be more productive to view oppressive social structures as a web that can work to our detriment or advantage, depending on our social location.

When I see myself the way the dominant culture sees me, I attempt to live up to its constructed stereotype of me. For example, as a poor preteen Latino living in New York City, I knew from a young age that I was different from the Euroamerican kids in my school and neighborhood. No matter how hard my parents tried to protect me from our poverty, they were unsuccessful. All I had to do was compare my life with the so-called typical family on the television show *Leave It to Beaver* to know that I was not normal. The images on the small screen were not my experience or reality, so something had to be wrong with me and my people. How else could I explain our poverty? Television and movies created a definition for me of what a Latino male is. Bombarded with media images of knife-wielding, oversexed, undereducated gang members, I attempted to live up to this image, obtaining and carrying a switchblade at the age of twelve and accepting poor grades as an inherited character flaw that came with being Hispanic. I saw myself the way Euroamericans saw me. I would pray that God would grant me blond hair and blue eyes. I even tried changing my name to Mike. With time, I looked toward the dominant Euroamerican culture in order to establish the standards for perfection in my own life. As to my own Hispanic roots, I viewed them with disdain, defining them in the same way that the dominant culture saw them. By seeing myself through the eyes of the dominant culture, I developed false consciousness, that is, a false way of self-perception, a way that was established early in my childhood.

A famous study conducted in 1984 to test racial self-identification illustrates the effects upon people of color who learn, as children, to see themselves through the eyes of the dominant culture. Thirty-five black males and twenty-three black females, ages four through six, were given two infant dolls, identical in every way except for skin color. One doll was white, the other was black. The children were asked which doll looked nice, which looked bad. Not surprisingly, the children preferred the white dolls, with boys more likely than girls wanting to identify with the white doll. The study concluded that because of the socioeconomic disadvantages associated with blackness, children were less willing to identify with that race.[10] From an early age, external social structures taught them that white is better. If double or multiple consciousness imposes upon people of color a self-image that is defined by the dominant culture, then how can they be liberated from this false consciousness?

The first act toward any form of liberation from oppressive structures is to see oneself through one's own eyes and define oneself through one's own terms. Rejecting how the dominant culture sees and defines people of color becomes in itself a consciousness-raising activity that allows those who are marginalized to define themselves apart from the negative stereotypes usually imposed. Learning to read the Bible from one's social location can become an integral part of this liberating process. Reading biblical texts from the underside of the U.S. culture empowers disenfranchised communities. Within the pages of the Bible, the marginalized discover a God who sides with those who are oppressed, actively leading them toward a promised land.

It would be erroneous to assume that the biblical interpretations arising from the margins of society are solely for the consumption of people of color. Because of the hermeneutical privilege of the oppressed, marginalized groups are in a better position to interpret the Bible than the dominant culture. But biblical interpretations that are developed from the margins contain truths that are not restricted solely to the disenfranchised. Within these interpretations the dominant culture can also discover liberation and salvation, because the oppressors, like those oppressed, are locked into a societal structure that prevents both sides from becoming all that God has intended creation to be: saved and liberated.

Why then are the biblical interpretations of the disenfranchised so important in fully understanding the Scriptures? It is because people of color know what it means to live in a Eurocentric society where their very survival requires them to learn how to navigate laws, customs, traditions, and idiosyncracies designed to protect the power and privilege of the dominant culture. Although people of color know what it means to be marginalized within a Euroamerican culture, those with power and privilege have no conception of what it means to belong to a disenfranchised group. In fact, most Euroamericans can achieve success without having to know anything about, or associate with, people on the margins. The same cannot be said if the roles were reversed. Because those who are marginalized know how to exist in both their world and the world where they lack a voice, they can bring an expanded and raised consciousness to the reading of the Bible.

THE CENTER-MARGIN DICHOTOMY

As the disenfranchised read the Bible from the margins, that is, from their social location, their empowering interpretation unmasks and critiques oppressive structures. Reading the Bible from the margins implies that at times the Bible is read *to* the center. Often in fact, the text is read from the social location of those who occupy the center of society, those with power and privilege. Hence, the Bible is read from the center toward the margins in order to teach those who are less fortunate what they must do to occupy privileged space. Yet Jesus's audience was primarily the outcasts of society. This is why it is important to understand the message of Jesus from the perspective of the disenfranchised. The marginalized of Jesus' time occupied the privileged position of being the first to hear and respond to the gospel. By making the disenfranchised recipients of the Good News, Jesus added a political edge to his message.

Jesus used parables that resonated with the lives of the poor, the tax collectors, the prostitutes—in short, the marginalized. God's self-revelation to humanity does not occur from the centers of world power but in the margins of society. It is not from the court of Pharaoh that God's laws are revealed to humanity but from their slaves. Nor does the incarnation occur in the imperial palace of Caesar, or to the household of the high priest in Jerusalem. Rather, God is made flesh among the impure Galileans, impure because they were seen by the center as half-breeds, from a territory peopled by Arabs, Greeks, Asians, Phoenicians, Syrians, and Jews, a region where the unclean Gentiles outnumbered the Jews.

Paul attests to this phenomenon in his first letter to the Corinthians when he writes:

> God chose the foolish things of the world so that the wise might be shamed, and God chose the weak things of the world so that God might shame the strong. God chose the lowborn of the world and those despised, and those who are nothing so that God can bring to nothing those that are. (1 Cor. 1:27–28)

Paul understood that the gospel message was dismissed by the center of society. The rejected stone became the cornerstone of the gospel, becoming a stumbling block for the builders who rejected it.

The fifteenth chapter of the Gospel of Luke clearly illustrates this point. The chapter contains three parables. The first parable is about the shepherd of a hundred sheep, who, losing one, leaves the other ninety-nine and searches for the one that is lost. The second parable tells of a woman with ten drachmas, who, upon losing one, lights a lamp and sweeps the house until she finds the lost coin. The last parable is the story of the prodigal son, who squanders his father's inheritance, only to return penniless and yet find acceptance in his father's house. When a party is thrown to rejoice in the prodigal son's return, the dutiful son who remained and stayed faithful to the father becomes angry that his disobedient brother is brought back into the fold.

Traditionally, Euroamericans have interpreted these three parables by emphasizing those whom they consider lost. God's everlasting mercy for the lost (sheep, coin, or son) becomes the focal point in reading and understanding these passages, encouraging those in the center to go out and evangelize the lost. But this reading masks why Jesus told the parables in the first place and to whom they were directed. Usually, when reading these parables, the first three verses of the chapter are skipped or ignored. "All the tax collectors and sinners were drawing near to [Jesus] to hear him. But the Pharisees and scribes murmured, saying, 'This one receives sinners and eats with them!' He spoke to them these parables" (Luke 15:1–3). Luke begins the chapter by stating that those who resided on the margins, the tax collectors and sinners, were coming to hear Jesus. Worse yet, they were eating with him. Now, for those in the center, the Pharisees (who were upwardly mobile) and scribes (learned men of the Law), those in the margins of society were considered to be the *am ha-ares*, literally, "the people of the land." With the exception of the tax collectors, who collaborated with the Roman imperialist powers in order to survive, the people of the land were composed of the vast majority of the poor, people devoid of any power or privilege. Along with the tax collectors they were looked down upon for not keeping the purity regulations, not because they did not want to but because they were too busy trying to survive.

Like today's people of color, the dominant culture saw them as impure, ignorant, and responsible for their own marginalization, in short, sinners. These outcasts flocked to the liberating Good News Jesus proclaimed. As Jesus proclaimed his message, those with power and privilege found their space challenged. After all, according to Jesus, the tax collectors and prostitutes were making their way into the kingdom of God before the religious center (Matt. 21:31).

The three parables recorded in Luke 15 were not voiced by Jesus for the benefit of the "unsaved," that is, the lost sheep, the lost coin, or the prodigal son; rather the parables were intended for the religious center, the Pharisees and scribes who were murmuring. It is to this group that Jesus narrates the three parables. Yet all too often, when the dominant culture interprets these same parables, it focuses on those of the margins, who are usually perceived as lost. But as Jesus reached out to the margins of society, the center became upset that its constructed religious views might become jeopardized with the inclusion of "the people of the land." They were concerned that the addition of these "undesirables" would pollute their theological perspectives and their ornate temples. Their disdain for the margins is best illustrated in the prayer of the Pharisee as recorded in Luke: "The Pharisee was standing, praying to himself these things: God, I thank you that I am not as the rest of men, rapacious, unjust, adulterers, *or even as this tax collector*. I fast twice a week and tithe everything I receive" (18:11–12; emphasis added). While I am not questioning the concern God has for the lost, we misinterpret these parables when we ignore the subject of the narratives. Jesus was challenging the center to make room for those residing on the margins not because those on the margins require tutelage but rather, like the Pharisees and scribes of old, because there is much that the center needs to learn from the disenfranchised.

During my seminary years, many Euroamerican churches wanted to offer me positions (at about a quarter of what other ministers were being paid) to start a Hispanic mission somewhere in the basement. There was a sincere desire to "reach out to the lost," but when these Latino/as came to the church, they were ushered to the fellowship hall, where they could worship among themselves. The hope was that they would form a missionary church, some place else. The message was clear: you are not welcomed in *our* sanctuary—get saved and move on!

It is always difficult for those at the center to listen to those who reside at the margins of society. The latter's interpretation of God's movement in the world challenges what society has always taught to be normative. Yet Jesus was able and willing to learn from the margins of his times. We sometimes forget that Jesus was human as well as divine. As a human, he had to learn how to overcome human frailties. As a child, Jesus had to learn how to walk, talk, and read. As an adult, he had to overcome the temptation of sin, specifically the human desire for fame and riches. Satan, according to Matthew 4:1–11, tempted Jesus with possessions (bread), privilege (jumping off the Temple and not being hurt because of who Christ is), and power (all the kingdoms of the earth). Although Jesus successfully rebuffed Satan while in the desert, it would be naive to assume that he was never again tempted. A careful reading of the Scriptures shows how he had to learn not to fall into future temptations.

Another opportunity to be tempted by Satan occurred when Jesus refused to minister to a marginalized woman. Matthew 15:21–28 recounts the story of a Canaanite woman who came to Jesus so that her daughter could be healed. The Canaanites were seen by the Jews in very much the same way people of color are today seen by some Euroamericans, as an inferior people, no better than dogs. When the Canaanite woman appealed to Jesus for help, the Lord responded by saying, "I was sent only to the lost sheep of the house of Israel. It is not good to take the bread of the children and throw it to the dogs." How many times have people of the margins heard similar remarks from Euroamericans? Jobs, educational opportunities, and social services are for "real" Americans. Instead of taking food away from the children of hard-working "Americans" to throw to the dogs, "they" should just go back to where they came from. Leticia Guardiola-Sáenz, interpreting the text from her social location, points out that this woman crosses the "border" not to worship her oppressor (Jesus) but to demand an equal place at the table of the Lord. She demands to be treated as an equal.[11]

Now, Jesus' response was typical for a person who was inculturated to believe in the superiority of his or her particular race.

Jesus learned from his culture the superiority of Judaism and the inferiority of non-Jews. However, Jesus was willing to learn from a "woman of color" and thus avoided falling into the temptation of perpetuating racism. The woman responded by saying, "For even the dogs eat the crumbs that fall from the table of their masters." Her remark shocked Jesus into realizing that faith was not contingent on a person's ethnicity. In fact, Jesus had to admit that this was a woman of great faith.

Up to this point, the gospel message was only for the Jews. In fact, Jesus restricts the spreading of the Good News to his own race. In Matthew 10:5, Jesus sends his twelve disciples on their first missionary venture. He clearly instructs them, "Do not turn your steps into other nations, nor into Samaritan cities; rather, go to the lost sheep of the house of Israel." Yet five chapters later, from the Canaanite margins of Jesus' society came the challenge that the gospel would no longer be the exclusive property of one ethnic group and would instead become available for all who believe. Jesus learned something about his mission from this woman. By the end of his ministry, when he gives the great commission, he commands his followers to go out to all nations, not just the people of Israel. Now, if Jesus is willing to learn something from the margins of society, shouldn't his church be willing to do likewise?

CHAPTER 2

Reading the Bible from the Center

According to the Bible, any child who disrespects his or her parents should be put to death. Leviticus reads, "Anyone who curses their father and mother shall surely be executed" (20:9). Now, as a parent of two preteen-agers, I confess that at times I am very tempted to take this command literally. Yet I wonder, if we were to read in the newspapers that a father killed his son or daughter for uttering a curse toward him and claimed the authority of Scripture as his defense, would good churchgoing Christians rally to his support? If not, why? Why can't a parent put a rebellious teenager to death in accordance with the Bible?

The next verse (Lev. 20:10) calls for the death sentence for anyone who commits adultery. Just think of the impact this would have on our national government! How many high-ranking government officials, TV evangelists, business leaders, and everyday common folk have fallen into this sin? The bloodbath that would have to occur to uphold this commandment is staggering. Additionally, Leviticus 24:16 makes the cursing of God's name a capital offense. Although I personally shudder every time I hear people using the name of the Lord in vain, is their death a fit punishment for their transgression? Would anyone be willing to argue for the death sentence for those who constantly damn the name of God? Likewise, according to Exodus 31:14–15, anyone who works on the Sabbath must be killed. Should we execute police officers, hospital personnel, or firefighters who work on Sundays? What about the waiter who serves you lunch after church? Should his or her tip be a death sentence for working on the Sabbath?

As much as we do not want to admit it, we all read biblical texts selectively. Few, if any, would insist that these "peccadillos" deserve death. Most of us simply choose to ignore or outright disobey the punishments associated with such passages. In effect, all who claim the authority of the Bible make a conscious or unconscious decision to follow some sections of the Scriptures literally while following others symbolically. In fact, if we were to follow literally everything within the biblical text, we would probably end up in jail. For example, Psalm 137:9 provides a paradigm for treating enemies: "Blessed is the one who seizes and dashes your little ones against the stone." How can we reconcile the loving mercy of Christ with the vengeance of smashing the infants of our enemies against stones? We are forced to a choose. Either we take the Bible literally and commit crimes against humanity by obeying the psalmist, or we begin to question how we read and interpret certain sections of the Bible.

How do such verses reflect the social location of those who first penned them? How do we interpret these verses for our time? Does it make a difference in the interpretations if you are the victors or the parents whose babies will be dashed against rocks? Can the biblical text be read objectively so as to discover how these troubling verses are to be applied in the twenty-first century?

As the previous chapter mentioned, everyone approaches the Bible from her or his particular social location. The idea of reading the text from a position of complete "objectivity" is a myth constructed to protect the privileged space of those with the power to legitimize their interpretations. Yet, when those who are marginalized read the biblical text with their own eyes, they find their pain within the biblical story. In using the Bible as a source of reconciliation, salvation, and liberation, those within the margins of society realize that the Bible has also been historically used as a source of alienation, damnation, and subjugation. It is not the Bible that saves but the justice-based actions (praxis) rooted in the reading of the Bible, a reading that liberates when done from a marginalized perspective. Such a reading moves one to think beyond the Bible as simply a text of rules dictated by a God that must be unquestionably obeyed. Social location plays a crucial role in the reading (and the original writing) of the text. When this reading is done by those struggling with oppressive structures, liberation from these same structures becomes the means by which all Christians can move beyond the perception of the Bible as simply a "rule book."

If reading a text implies its application, then those who are disenfranchised, those who live in the underside of Euroamerican history, are the ones who can hear God's words in the context of their own suffering, making their oppressed existence part of the text's interpretation. Such a reading provides a fuller revelation of the Scriptures, a revelation that remains obscure to the dominant culture. Because they have learned how to function in a vulnerable realm constructed by those with power and privilege, they know more about the overall Euroamerican existence, which includes the sphere occupied by the dominant culture, than those with power know about their lives as subjugated "others." This does not confer truth exclusively on the oppressed. It only states that they are in a better position to understand the biblical call for justice than those who deceive themselves into thinking justice already exists.

If reading the Bible from the margins provides a closer understanding of the gospel message, then how is the Bible read from the center, from within the dominant power structures? How is the Bible constructed to justify oppressive structures that protect the power and privilege of the center at the expense of the margins? At the very least, how is the Bible understood so as to encourage the dominant culture to remain complicit with racism, classism, and sexism? Before we can begin to understand how the margins find their liberation and salvation within the biblical text, we must first explore how the text is used to justify the oppression and damnation of those who are disenfranchised.

A PRIVILEGED READING

When we read the Bible, we read it from our social location, a reading that usually justifies our lifestyle even if, at times, our lifestyle contradicts the very essence of the gospel message. Historically, the Bible has been used to justify such acts as genocide, slavery, war, crusades, colonialism, economic plunder, and gender oppression. Bible verses were quoted, sermons preached from pulpits, and theses written in theological academic centers to justify barbaric acts that were labeled "Christian missionary zeal" or "righteous indignation." Millions have unjustly died and perished in the name of Jesus and by the hands of those who call themselves his followers. In fact, one of the slave ships responsible for bringing

Africans to the Americas was named the *Jesus*. Although I do not wish to enter into a discussion concerning the personal "spiritual" fervor of such individuals, I do question how they reconciled the Bible with their oppressive acts. For example, how could "Christian" slave masters during the antebellum period inflict unbearable misery upon other human beings, day in and day out, and still be able to sing God's praises and proclaim God's everlasting mercy on Sunday mornings? How is the love of Christ reconciled with the inhumanity of some of his self-proclaimed followers today who benefit from social structures designed to increase their status at others' expense? In other words, how do they read the Bible from the center of power and privilege?

The Age of Enlightenment is crucial in understanding how the dominant Eurocentric culture reads the Bible. The Enlightenment was an eighteenth-century intellectual movement prevalent throughout western Europe. Centuries of bloody religious conflicts following the Protestant Reformation of the early 1500s, coupled with the rise of science, led thinkers of the Enlightenment to construct a new worldview based on human reason and understanding. Philosophical rationalism gained ascendancy, deriving its methodologies from science and natural philosophy. A major objective of this project was to replace religion, the source of so much human misery, with science. Science became the new means for knowing nature and the destiny of humans. In short, science was looked to as the salvation of humanity. The intolerance of the established Christian churches, which had led to centuries of religious warfare, was associated with a premodern worldview where the answer to every question of the universe was believed to reside in the Bible. The new "modern" worldview replaced the Bible with human reason and science.

While all Christian groups reject the total replacement of religion with science, the tension created by modernity continues to exist. For example, throughout the United States today, state legislatures and local school boards attempt to include creationism (a literal reading of Genesis 1) within the school curricula, to be taught alongside evolutionary theory. This tension, played out in the political sphere, bears witness to the continuous impact of the Enlightenment. An endeavor to reconcile the Bible with science in order to create a harmonious worldview is undertaken by many scholars within academia. Yet putting God under a microscope makes the Bible into a science book as discussions develop over the meaning of the word "day" in the creation story. Was a day twenty-four hours, or was a day a million years?

What I find interesting is that most biblical scholars from the margins of society usually do not participate in such debates. When people live under oppressive structures, they turn to the Bible for the strength to survive another day, not to figure out how long a day lasted in Genesis 1. The Bible is not read with the intellectual curiosity of solving cosmic mysteries; rather, most people on the margins look to the text to find guidance in dealing with daily life, a life usually marked by struggles and hardships. Debates over the scientific validity of the Scriptures become a luxurious privilege for those who do not endure oppressive and discriminating structures. For the dominant culture, the objective in reading the Bible is to answer such questions. Regardless of the answer, whether it appeals to the fundamentalists or the liberals, the overall dominant culture reads the text through the lens of modernity, even while protesting the present-day ramifications of the Enlightenment.

Does God exist? becomes the overall quest of those residing within the dominant culture. In contrast, from the margins of society the question becomes, What is the character of this God that we claim exists? While the center's evangelistic mission is to convince the nonbeliever to believe, those who reside on the underside of society see their evangelistic venture to be that of convincing the nonperson of his or her humanity based on the image of God that dwells within them. Because those at the center ask different questions than those who reside on the margins of society, the Bible provides different answers. The dominant culture usually looks for answers to questions that are simply unimportant to the social location of those living under oppressive structures. For example, a student once asked me if I supported prayer in schools. The class was at first shocked by my reply. I said I supported books, computers, and microscopes in schools, because the schools within the *barrios* and ghettos of this country lack these basic necessities, which are needed to equip children from the margins to compete in the global marketplace. Prayer in schools becomes a luxury debated in those predominantly white school systems that have already obtained all that is necessary in providing their children with a competitive education.

A Biblical Paradigm for Justifying Privilege

Besides reading the Bible to answer questions of little use to those who are marginalized, the center also reads the Bible in such a way that its power and privilege remain justified by the biblical text. Such a reading is based on the reader's self-centeredness. Self-centeredness begins with the fall of humanity, the original disobedience of Adam and Eve. In their act of eating the forbidden fruit, the mango, from the tree of the knowledge of good and evil, they committed sin, a sin rooted in the central idea of usurping God's authority as Creator.[1] The original sin of humanity is the pride of attempting to become "like gods" (Gen. 3:5). Self-centeredness is the endeavor of replacing God with humans, expressed today as the drive for power and privilege. Through unlimited power and privilege, those in the center with sufficient economic privilege have the opportunity of becoming gods, usually at the expense of those who live in the periphery of society.

For example, due to the high consumption of grain-fed livestock by residents of the United States, enough food is consumed by them to feed over a billion people in poor countries. According to Oxford economist Donald Hay, a mere 2 percent of the world's grain harvest is sufficient, if shared, to eliminate world hunger and malnutrition. Yet, ironically, in a world where over thirty-four thousand children die each day of hunger and preventable diseases, the number of overweight adults in the United States increased from 26 to 34 percent between 1988 and 1991. The United States, the world's center, consumes so much of the world's resources that its people now spend billions of dollars annually trying to lose weight in a world where the majority of its inhabitants go to bed hungry. In fact, the dollar value of the food thrown into North American garbage cans each year equals one-fifth of the total annual income of all the Christians living in Africa.[2] This self-centeredness believes in its moral right to accumulate while others go hungry, never connecting the relationship between having and not having. The accumulation of wealth is understood as the product of "hard work."

The sharing of goods and possessions, each according to his or her needs, is usually attributed to Karl Marx, and most Christians believe this phrase to be a Marxist dictum. In reality, it is a biblical principle for the Christian church, one established early in its formation. The book of Acts states, "And the believers together, holding all things in common, sold their goods and possessions and distributed them to all, according to each one's need" (2:44–45). Yet this concept, dangerously reminiscent of some type of socialism, is rejected by those of us who live in a capitalist society, because we have been taught that communism/socialism is evil or possibly that it is a good idea that simply does not work. Our capitalist system takes precedence; we rarely think of how those who are economically disenfranchised understand passages like the one found in Acts 2.

In spite of the dominant culture's rhetoric of succeeding through hard work, seldom have the rich or powerful worked as hard as a migrant laborer. Picking blueberries, cucumbers, or onions is harsh, backbreaking work, but it is not enough to advance economically because compensations fall way below the minimum wage. Adults and their children (who should be in school) work in the fields for long hours and barely gain enough funds to maintain a household. Even if they were paid minimum wages, their income would still fall $5,000 below the 1998 poverty line. Their economic oppression secures low prices for fresh fruits and vegetables, making consumers of these produce complicit with their exploitation.

Migrant workers, barely existing on the margins of society, are also needed as a reserve army of disposable laborers to keep wages depressed so that the benefits are passed on to the company owners or the corporate officers and their stockholders. Whether we wish to admit it or not, a segment of the population must be kept in a state of financial submission in order for the overall economy to function at top efficiency. This segment is usually composed of people on the margins, who are disproportionately overrepresented in unemployment figures. Like the migrant workers, they are defined by the dominant culture as people holding our community back, looking for a handout, and using up *our* social services. The center remains complicit with economic structures that require a segment of the population to remain in poverty so that the dominant culture can benefit from lower grocery bills and so that these savings can be diverted to some of life's necessities, like a bigger house or a luxury car. Our having is possible because the migrant workers, and others like them, have not. And our willingness to maintain the status quo, which allows the center to benefit from the sweat of the marginalized labor, is testimony to our self-centeredness.

Of course, self-centeredness is not limited to the center's relationship with migrant workers. The dominant culture benefits and advances in society simply because it belongs to the center. A sweeping five-year study released in October 1999 concluded that skin color remains a major factor in determining economic success within the United States. The seven-volume survey, focusing on Boston, Atlanta, Detroit, and Los Angeles, studied job market participation, racial inequality, and political attitudes among 9,000 households and 3,500 employers. The fifty researchers discovered that race continues to be deeply entrenched in determining success within the United States even though many within the dominant culture fail to realize this or are unwilling to admit it. The study revealed the pervasiveness of racist structures, from highly segregated housing to labor markets that hire one racial group over another, with people of color detrimentally affected.[3] The bottom line: whiteness is a social privilege that provides opportunities for housing, jobs, and markets unavailable to most people on the margins. Success within the United States may have more to do with white skin pigmentation than "hard work."

Additionally, whiteness protects violators of the law from being punished as severely as nonwhites. According to a ninety-page report released by the Leadership Conference on Civil Rights, a Washington, D.C.–based civil-rights coalition, justice and skin pigmentation continue to remain linked. Titled "Justice on Trial: Racial Disparities in the American Criminal Justice System," the report found that 1) 74 percent of all those who are deported by the INS are of Mexican origin even though less than half of all undocumented people are from Mexico; 2) Latino/as are likely to be released in only 26 percent of their legal cases while non-Hispanics are released before trial 66 percent of the time; and 3) blacks who kill whites were sentenced to death twenty-two times more frequently than blacks who kill blacks and seven times more frequently than whites who kill blacks. Additionally, black youths are six times more likely to be imprisoned than white youths, even when charged with similar crimes and when neither has a prior record.[4]

Self-centeredness, as the sin of pride, pursues power and privilege at the expense or detriment of others in its attempt to replace God with the self. Yet no one is willing to admit one's own self-centeredness. Instead, most wish to proclaim their self-righteousness. Here is a dialectical conflict. How do well-meaning Christians read the Bible in order to reconcile a faith in Christ with their continuous pursuit of power and privilege? In other words, how is the Bible read to justify living amid wealth and privilege while others lack basic rights and necessities?

The following example may help answer these questions. In reading the Gospels, we discover that Jesus spoke a great deal about money, our relationship to money, and the different relationships money creates. In fact, he mentions this subject more than he does heaven, the Spirit, God's kingdom, or his own messiahship. Jesus refers to money more than any other topic, clearly showing that he knew where our treasures lay. According to Matthew, Jesus provides his would-be followers with a clear choice: "No one is able to serve two lords. For they will either hate the one and love the other, or they will cleave to one and despise the other. You are not able to serve God and Mammon" (6:24). "Mammon" is an Aramaic word for wealth, money, or property. Here is the choice Jesus gives us: we can pursue self-centeredness and the power and privilege it provides or we can choose to follow God, but we can't do both. Nonetheless, those at the center, accustomed to its privilege, want to do both. And they believe that it is possible to serve God and to protect their power and privilege. This pursuit of power and wealth, masked under a facade of Christianity, inevitably leads to injustice, here defined as the undue privilege obtained by the powerful and the lack of rights existing for the powerless.

Rationalizing injustices allows those at the center to continue benefiting at the expense of the margins while simultaneously defining themselves as good Christians. Their power and privilege are justified as something earned purely through the sweat of their brow. This rationalization can take the form of ideology. For example, in capitalism the ideology of "the survival of the fittest" dismisses those who reside in the underside of capitalism as not being fit to survive. Their poverty becomes proof of their deserved marginality. The success of the center is attributed to its ingenuity and hard work. If the disenfranchised were not so lazy or were smarter, then they too could earn a slice of the American pie.

Ideologies provide simple answers to inequalities by laying the blame of marginality upon the victims of oppressive structures. This type of ideology also contributes to the rise of stereotyping. If the exclusive neighborhoods are predominantly white while the economically deprived areas are mainly composed of people of color, if those who occupy positions in top management and U.S. corporate boardrooms are white males while those who occupy the menial positions are women and people on the margins, and if our prison systems remain disproportionately composed of nonwhite males, the center can only conclude that people on the margins are lazy and so live in the ghettos and *barrios,* that women and minorities are less intelligent and so occupy servile jobs, and that nonwhite males are dangerous and wicked creatures deserving incarceration.

While disenfranchised groups see unjust social structures, those who benefit from those structures fail or refuse to recognize the status quo as oppressive; here lies a major division between U.S. citizens. Yet, when those who benefit from unjust structures are able to make their perspectives normative due to the power of the center, they create a worldview that demands biblical justification in order to avoid any incongruency between what they believe and what they do. The unchecked power of the dominant culture that resides in the center of society provides the privilege of defining and determining how the Bible is read and interpreted. Hence, what develops is an attempt to read the Bible to redefine or to justify the unjust privileges of the center. Reading the Bible to justify one's social location imprisons the text by spiritualizing reality and thus obscuring or hiding it. This results in a culture of silence prevailing where the interpretation of the center is neither questioned nor challenged.

The danger for those on the margins is that they will read the Bible through the eyes of elite white males and convince themselves of the justice of their own oppression. Unaware of the reasons for their marginalization, those who are disenfranchised often accept the order of things that relegates them to be exploited. Yet, as those on the margins begin to claim the biblical text as their own, their reading shifts to a social location of the margins. Such a reading threatens what has been constructed by the center as the normative interpretation and threatens the very social structures that create oppression.

Reading the Bible to justify one's social location results in a spiritual or metaphoric reading of the biblical text rather than a material reading. A metaphoric reading is the process of interpreting the biblical text in such a way that its call for action becomes an intention or conviction of the heart rather than physical action to be undertaken. A material reading, on the other hand, attempts to introduce the reality of daily struggles into the Bible. Close attention is given to how the social location of the marginalized, both today and during biblical times, affects how the Bible should be understood.

For example, for many within the center, the entire message and purpose of the Bible can be reduced to the biblical verse found in John 3:16: "For God so loved the world that God gave God's only begotten Son, so that everyone believing in him may not perish but have life everlasting." It is not uncommon to see someone holding up a poster sign at a televised sporting event with simply "John 3:16" written upon it. Yet most who are marginalized look to Luke 4:18–19. In these verses, Luke records the first sermon Jesus ever gave, a sermon that is interpreted as the foundation of the gospel message, in effect Jesus' mission statement for action. In these verses, Jesus says, "The Spirit of the Lord is on me, therefore the Spirit anointed me to preach the gospel to the poor. The Spirit has sent me to heal the brokenhearted, to preach liberation to the captives, and new sight to the blind, to set those who are oppressed free, and to preach an acceptable year of the Lord." In this passage, Jesus singles out those who are poor as the recipients of the Good News. The gospel is for those who are poor and oppressed, and through them the message is extended toward those who profit from the marginalized.

Jesus is quoting the prophet Isaiah (61:1–2), who wrote about the physical captivity and oppression of the Israelites. In Jesus' mission statement, he refers to the physical problems of those who reside on the margins of society. A metaphoric reading would avoid Jesus' clear intention by interpreting his words to mean that all are poor *in spirit*, hence all are in need of the Good News. Even the rich, those with power and privilege who benefit at the expense of the marginalized, can be defined as poor, thus avoiding any possible responsibility or obligation toward those whom Jesus called poor. While the need of those in the center to hear the Good News is not denied, the radicalness of Jesus' words is to make those in the margins the recipients of the gospel, and the periphery of society the social location from where the gospel is defined and understood. Yet, when this radicalness is moderated by defining the center as "poor in spirit," then the mandate to correct unjust structures that create poverty is watered down.

When those in the center read the Bible to justify privilege, they are not satisfied with simply rationalizing their own social location. A desire also exists to define their power and privilege as a blessing from God, given because of their moral righteousness. When some evangelical Christians see a homeless person, usually their first reaction is to witness God's salvation to them. The homeless person becomes an object for conversion. For this reason, many Christian homeless shelters require the participants to hear a sermon before they are fed. If their souls can be saved, then God will bless them with material possessions. Direct action toward social justice (works) is minimized in favor of right belief (doctrine). Only the latter can save.

While there is no denying that some poverty is caused by wrong choices, specifically drug and alcohol abuse, in many cases substance abuse is a means of escaping the hopelessness of existing on the margins of society. What can be expected when children living in the ghettos and *barrios* are forced to attend deteriorating school buildings without adequate books and supplies while the schools in the white neighborhoods on the other side of town have the latest technology needed to make their students competitive in a global marketplace? This inequality in educational opportunities is one of the factors eventually contributing to unemployment and homelessness. Unjust social structures also affect the ability to acquire adequate employment. For example, it took unskilled, unemployed whites in Detroit, representative of the rest of the nation's major cities, approximately 91 hours to generate a job offer, while it took unskilled, unemployed blacks 167 hours to obtain a similar offer.[5] Social forces such as these produce opportunities for one segment of society and deny them to another. When this lack of opportunities leads to poverty, specifically in the extreme form of homelessness, the center rationalizes its privilege by blaming the victims for their poverty. An extreme form of justifying the center's "blessings" is a religious ideology known as prosperity theology. Simply stated, prosperity theology maintains that Christians are "children" of the King. Their Creator wants only the best for God's children and is ready to materially bless them *if* they have enough faith.

To read the Bible from the center, from a social location of power and privilege, is to use the Bible to justify a lifestyle constructed through opportunities denied to most people on the margins. For some Christians from the center of power and privilege, the Bible is often read to uncover its mysteries, debate issues such as creationism versus evolution, or advocate personal salvation. Missing is any substantial discourse on sin as manifested in the social structures that create undue privilege for the center and a lack of rights for the powerless. Reading the Bible from the margins moves the discourse toward a concrete community-based plan of action.

Pitfalls in Raising Consciousness

Learning to read the Bible from the margins liberates the center from using the Bible to justify its privilege and power. Yet the raising of consciousness for the center does not automatically insure that these Christians will participate in actions that liberate the disenfranchised. In fact, several pitfalls exist when the center's consciousness is raised yet people do nothing to change oppressive structures.

For example, when those at the center realize that their reading of the Bible does not justify their privileged space, they may experience anguish and dismay, but these feelings are insufficient to establish a more just social order. At times, the center, motivated by guilt, may begin to make those who are marginalized the object of their humanitarianism. Through charities or false generosity, those of the center may attempt to mentor those they consider less fortunate, still refusing to connect their own "having" with the "not having" of the disenfranchised. But the marginalized neither need nor require pity from the center or its models for emulation.

What is required for the salvation of the center and for the creation of a just society is the radical commitment to be in solidarity with those who exist on the margins of society and to accompany them in their daily struggle. This does not mean approaching the margins to lead them out of their oppression but to be in solidarity and to serve them as they formulate their own actions for liberation. Solidarity is no easy task because those at the center are often unable to free themselves from their former prejudices. These prejudices can include suspicion about the ability of the disenfranchised to think for themselves, to understand how oppressive power structures work, or to figure out how best to overcome these structures.

WORDS OF CONCERN

Traditionally, disenfranchised groups have constructed well-defined categories as to who are the perpetrators and the victims of injustices. All too often, people on the margins tend to identify the oppressive structures of the dominant Eurocentric culture while overlooking those within their own marginalized community. Yet within the space of disenfranchised groups, intrastructures of oppression also exist.

Additionally, there is a real and present danger of romanticizing the social location of the marginalized. Their hermeneutical privilege can absolutize radical actions inconsistent with the biblical text but nonetheless perceived as a necessary process toward liberation. In effect, the Bible may simply baptize whatever actions originate or are initiated within the margins of society. Such a reading falls into the peril of confusing subjectivity for objectivity, where the Scriptures are interpreted to justify positions and strategies that may promise immediate liberation from oppressive social structures but, in the long run, may simply replace those in power with a new group, never dealing with the oppressive structures themselves.

For example, what happens when historically oppressed groups obtain financial success? In reading the Bible from the margins, readers must guard against becoming themselves suboppressors by surmounting the structures of oppression rather than dismantling them. When historically marginalized groups are taught how to read the Bible and define social structures from the perspectives of the dominant culture, the possibility exists that if they gain some power, they might in turn use the oppressive structures as their model. Equality with white upper-class males becomes confused with the goal of liberation. Liberation is thus understood as equality with white elite males, even though the space occupied by these elite white males requires the oppression of some other group to maintain their power and privilege.[6]

Another similar concern to be avoided is the temptation to equalize all forms of marginality. In an attempt to create solidarity among marginalized communities, at times intrastructures of oppression are avoided or ignored. For example, among Hispanics, some privilege exists for those who do not have pronounced Amerindian or African features. Additionally, ethnic discrimination is evident between Cubans and Puerto Ricans, Mexicans and Central Americans, Chileans and Argentinians, and any other combination. The same can be said about ethnic discrimination within Asian communities, as in the case of Japanese, Koreans (North or South), Vietnamese, and Chinese, just to name a few. Among African Americans, those with lighter skin pigmentation usually benefit more from society than those who are darker. If whiteness is defined as ultimate perfection, then those who are closest to being white obtain some privilege denied their darker compatriots. One must also add to this mix patriarchal structures and homophobic tendencies in all of these traditionally marginalized groups. In effect, a web of oppression exists that at times privileges a section of the marginalized.

Like the dominant culture, marginalized communities must apply a hermeneutics of suspicion; that is, they must also be suspicious of how they interpret the Bible and be fully aware of how their own social location influences their interpretations. The salient individualism prevalent within the dominant culture must be avoided lest the Bible become a source that confirms one's own ideology. Reading the Bible within the faith community helps avoid the temptation of an individualistic reading of self-justification that justifies whatever one is doing.

For this reason, it is crucial to hear the testimonies of our elders, who are often ignored by our culture but mightily used by the Spirit of God to reveal God's will. The experience of most faith communities is that the greatest wisdom appears to emanate from these elders of the church, rather than professors, seminary-educated pastors, deacons, or other ministers who are at times chosen for these positions because of their standing in the overall community. Latina theologian Elizabeth Conde-Frazier illustrates how matriarchs in particular become modern prophets of God's word to those who are abused. She speaks of a woman of faith in her seventies by the name of Doña Inez. One day a woman, who bore the evidence of physical abuse, came to a Bible study in which Doña Inez was participating. Doña Inez caressed the abused woman, attempting to soothe her body and spirit. Finally, in a public whisper, she said,

> Because the Bible says that what we loose on earth will be loosed in heaven and what we bind on earth will be bound in Heaven, in the name of Jesus I loose you from your bonds to this man who has done this to you. You are not guilty of anything he has done. Go now to your cousin's house and start a new life. Don't look back or go back like Lot's wife. In God's name, we will provide for you all your needs.[7]

Her words not only set this oppressed woman free but also bound the rest of the faith community to support and provide for her.

SEARCHING FOR THE ABUNDANT LIFE

This chapter has explored how the Bible is read by those who benefit from oppressive social structures to justify their privilege. Some biblical verses have been misinterpreted, consciously or unconsciously, to protect the power and privilege of the dominant culture. Other verses seem to imply the sanctification of non-Christian actions such as ethnic cleansing. How then can Christians complicit in the oppression of their neighbors continue to rely on the authority of Scripture as the basis for Christian ethics? What type of morality can the faith community claim?

It is important to remember that the biblical text is the witness of God's revelation to humanity, a book designed to point the reader to the Deity. But is the Bible the fullest revelation of God to humanity? No, Jesus is the fullest revelation of God to humanity. The Bible bears witness to that revelation and as such becomes the basis of faith for the community of believers. Yet it is important to acknowledge that the Bible is written from within the social location of different writers. While this multitude of writers spanning centuries all proclaim the same revelation of God's love and mercy, a love and mercy that find ultimate manifestation in the incarnation, these writers were born into, and were greatly influenced by, their social environments. Their writings assumed the normative oppressive structures of their times, structures we clearly repudiate today. Does this invalidate the Bible? No! But it clearly places a greater responsibility on the reader to interpret the text in light of the life, death, and resurrection of Christ.

How then do those of the faith community read the Bible, still claiming authority for their lives yet rejecting the passages that appear to call for the death of others? Readers should always submit their interpretation to the Holy Spirit, reading the text within the marginalized body of faith and remaining always cognizant of the basic purpose of the gospel. Jesus Christ, in the Gospel of John, said it best: "I came that they may have life, and have it abundantly" (10:10).

Simply put, if a biblical interpretation prevents life from being lived abundantly by a segment of the population or, worse, if it brings death, then it is anti-gospel. When a reading of the Bible ignores how minority groups are denied access to opportunities, when the Bible is read to rationalize the riches of the center while disregarding the plight of the poor, and when reading the Bible vindicates the relegation of women to second-class status, then such interpretations cease to be biblically based. Only interpretations that empower all elements of humanity, offering abundant life in the here-now, as opposed to just the here-after, are biblically sound.

Jesus Christ and his life-giving mission become the lens by which the rest of the biblical text is interpreted. During the Sermon on the Mount, as found in Matthew 5–7, Jesus reinterprets the Hebrew Scriptures to bring them in line with the gospel message, clearly telling his followers to reject passages that bring subjugation or death to others. Specifically, Jesus said in Matthew, "You heard that it was said, 'An eye for an eye and a tooth for a tooth.' But I say to you, do not resist evil, but whoever strikes you on your right cheek, turn to him the other" (5:38–39). According to Jesus, the biblical mandate of Exodus 21:24, which literally calls for "an eye for an eye and a tooth for a tooth," had to be rejected by his followers. In short, Jesus is calling his disciples to renounce a segment of Scripture!

These so-called laws of retaliation, known as the *lex talionis,* were never intended to require vengeance but, rather, to restrict it. Yet Jesus does away with the whole concept of revenge by calling his followers to a higher standard in interpreting the Hebrew Bible. Instead, the disciple of Christ is required to express the unconditional love of God. The formerly accepted biblical interpretation that sanctioned limited retributive vengeance was replaced with a new interpretation that mirrored the life and mission of Christ. In this same spirit, those who have historically suffered under the dominant culture's interpretations of the Bible question, as did Jesus, normative interpretations of the text and, at times, the passages themselves if the end results bring oppression and deny "life abundance."

How do we know if an interpretation or a passage is responsible for creating oppressive structures? By recognizing that at times individuals have no choice but to choose among options that are all unsatisfactory. For example, most Christians agree that they should not lie. Nevertheless, Exodus 1:15–22 recounts the story of two midwives who were commanded by the pharaoh to kill all the male children born to the Israelites. The midwives, however, disobeyed the pharaoh because they "feared God." When questioned as to why they defied the pharaoh, they lied, stating that Hebrew women were more vigorous than Egyptian women and gave birth before the midwives were able to attend them. Even though they lied to the pharaoh, Exodus states, "And God dealt well with the midwives" (1:20).

If the Bible is read as a book of regulations that clearly determine right and wrong, then passages like this one in Exodus become difficult to understand. If lying is always wrong, how then can God bless these two women for lying? Absolute truths derived from the Bible become somewhat problematic. Often, such absolutes become one of the privileges of those who are sheltered from the harshness of oppressive structures. Like the midwives, people who live under oppressive structures often find themselves in situations where decisions aren't easy or obvious and may even contradict supposed biblical principles. Many times the only choice available is the one in which a "lesser" evil is chosen. Yes, the midwives could have told the truth, but they would have been killed for disobeying the pharaoh, and someone else would have been found to carry out the pharaoh's wishes; or they could have lied and continued to save as many Hebrew boys as possible. Both killing and lying are vices to be avoided, but in this case, lying had the potential to save lives, and in the end Moses grew up to be used by God to liberate God's chosen people.

Being caught between two sinful choices due to the overall structures of oppression can also be illustrated in the story of Doña Inez presented earlier. Doña Inez told the battered wife to leave her abusive husband. According to Malachi 2:16, God hates divorce. This oppressed woman—and her community of faith— was forced to make one of two choices, both of which were bad. Either she divorced her husband or she continued to live in submission to an abusive situation. Those who know what it means to live within a marginalized space, like Doña Inez, who suffered under both ethnic discrimination and sexism, can be effective guides for others who face oppression. At times, the only way to choose is to pick the action that most closely resembles the purpose of Jesus, who "came that they may have life, and have it abundantly."

All biblical interpretations, to a greater or lesser degree, are subjective. None of us comes to the Bible objectively. Someone, usually someone we love and respect, like our parents, our pastor, or a teacher, has interpreted the text for us. Our love and affection for these persons are manifested by accepting their interpretations. Yet it is important to question interpretations that justify unjust social structures, specifically in the area of racism, classism, and sexism. Before exploring how the Bible is read from the margins so as to claim the liberative message of the gospel, it will be helpful to see how the center has historically read the Bible to justify race, class, and gender oppression. It is important to note that while these three forms of oppression are examined separately, in reality they are intertwined. Race, class, and gender oppressions are the three prongs of "Satan's" pitchfork.

CHAPTER 3

Unmasking the Biblical Justification
of Racism and Classism

He was a young African man from Zimbabwe named John, a new immigrant to the United States. I met John in a Bible class I was teaching at a predominantly African and African American church in Yeadon, Pennsylvania, where my family and I chose to worship. I was doing a series on how the Bible has been used to justify race, class, and gender oppression. I challenged my fellow congregants to read the Bible from their particular social location, using their cultural symbols to understand the mysteries of God and hear the voice of God's Spirit. After the class, John approached me. He was perplexed at my insistence that he should attempt to understand God through his own culture. He said that when he became a Christian, the missionary told him that he now had to adopt a "Christian" name. At first I did not understand what he meant. But the more we talked, I began to realize that John was not his birth name. Becoming a Christian meant that he had to disassociate with his "pagan" African past, including his birth name. I asked him what his real name was. He replied, "Ruvimbo." I then told him that Ruvimbo is indeed his Christian name and John is his pagan name. I could see the confusion in his eyes—after all, I was challenging the worldview he was taught by those responsible for his Christianization. Besides, he had already legally changed his name to John.

As the months went by, whenever I saw him, I made it a point to call him Ruvimbo. One day, he was in a crowd of friends, all from different African nations yet all having European names. "Hello, Ruvimbo, how are you doing?" I asked. He replied that he was fine. All of his friends looked at me in shock. One of them then said to Ruvimbo, "How weird to hear your African name being used in church." I walked away saddened. The imposition of the European way of seeing oneself has created a false consciousness that has been so legitimized and normalized in these young African minds that to see or refer to themselves as African has become "weird." They have learned to see themselves through the eyes of those who would have them believe that being African is mutually exclusive to being Christian. Those at the margins of society have been taught to believe that to be Christian means to become Eurocentric, not just in name but, more important, in thought. The clear implication is that the Bible can be understood only through a Eurocentric culture.

What is called "objective" biblical interpretation is, in fact, subjective, a product of the social location of the interpreter. If the interpreter is a Euroamerican male with economic privilege, then the Eurocentric viewpoint becomes the obvious way of reading the Bible. In the past, and even today, it then becomes the universal way of interpreting the text, and interpretations from different cultures are measured by how close they come to the Eurocentric ideal. When the interpretations from the center become confused with biblical truths, questioning interpretations that justify racism, classism, and sexism appears to be a critique of the biblical text itself, something no "true" Christian would dare to do. Those who question certain interpretations constructed within the center of society are charged with being nonbiblical. These next two chapters will explore how the Bible has been and is used and abused to normalize race, class, and gender oppression. Additionally, we will look to some oppressed communities to see how they are able to reclaim the text as a source of their own liberation. We will attempt to discover how Ruvimbo, and so many others like him, can read the Bible through their own eyes so that their faith can lead them to an abundant life in God, beholden to no one except the Creator of all things.

JUSTIFYING RACISM

How has the Bible been read to justify the social structures of racism? How has the white center interpreted the Bible to justify unequal opportunities? How is the message of belonging to the heavenly body of Christ reconciled with the exclusion of certain individuals from the earthly church body due to their skin pigmentation? Before answering these questions, let us examine a hymn about the slain Lamb of God from the book of Revelation:

> After I saw these things, I looked and saw a great crowd, impossible to number, out of every tribe, language, people, and nation, standing before the throne and before the Lamb, clothed in white robes with palms in their hands. And they cry with a great voice saying, "Salvation to our God sitting on the throne, and to the Lamb!" (7:9–10)

In this passage, the author, John, has a vision of the kingdom of heaven in all its glory, as the hosts of heaven surround the throne of God. Those who are encircling the throne are so great in number that it becomes impossible to count them. John is impressed with the strength of their collective voices as they sing about God's victories. In this song, Christ's mission of creating a multicultural church is professed, a church ransomed from "every tribe, language, people, and nation." What John witnessed is the heavenly model for Christians waiting to enter glory. This glimpse of heavenly worship becomes the model by which churches should pattern earthly worship.

This pattern began during the Pentecost event at the start of the Christian movement. According to Acts 2:4–11, Peter, full of the Holy Spirit, addressed the crowd that had gathered "from every nation" outside the house where the disciples met. Amazingly, each person heard the message in his or her own language. The miracle of Pentecost is not that the crowd representing various nations understood the language spoken by Peter but, rather, that they heard the message in their own tongue. The Genesis story concerning the tower of Babel (Gen. 11:1–9) is reversed. In the Genesis story, diverse languages are used to separate people. Now the ushering in of God's Spirit unifies God's people, transcending the earlier separation. As a result, three thousand were converted, representing Parthians, Medes, Elamites, Mesopotamians, Judeans, Cappadocians, Pontusians, Asians, Phrygians, Pamphylians, Egyptians, Libyans, Cyrenes, Romans, Cretans, and Arabs, all of whom represented the first Christian church, a very multicultural church. Hence, from Acts to Revelation, from the alpha to the omega, the ideal Christian church, as the body of Christ, is multicultural.

Now look at today's churches. Are the parishioners from "every tribe, language, people, and nation?" If not, why? Is homogeneity caused by racism, whether historical or contemporary? If you live in a culturally diverse city or town yet everyone in church looks the same and the diversity of the body of Christ is not reflected in the body of believers, then the church has failed to emulate what it is called to be, usually because it is a product or a victim of racism.

In the book of Revelation, the angel tells John, "You must again prophesy about many tribes, languages, peoples, and nations" (10:11). In the past, it was understood that the "white man's burden" was to bring civilization to the margins, a civilization that includes the gospel message. The message went from the center to the margins via missionaries and evangelists. Yet here the angel is telling John to go to the center, his Jewish community, and tell them *about* the margins. The center incorrectly assumes that its task is to bring the gospel to the margins. How do we reach *them*? What must we do to bring *them* into the fold? What programs must we initiate so as to bring *them* under our tutelage? In reality, the gospel is thriving in the margins of society. The real question facing the center, accustomed to confusing its interpretations with the biblical text itself, is whether those at the center will also participate in the body of Christ that already exists in the margins of society.[1]

Beyond the Black-and-White Dichotomy

Throughout the South during the first half of the twentieth century, public signs indicated what was reserved for the center and what was designated for the margins. The words "White" and "Colored" appeared on signs that segregated society, placing restrictions on where African Americans in particular, and people of color in general, could eat, sleep, drink, sit, live, work, and walk. What was overtly proclaimed in the South was subtly enforced in the North. What Malcolm X called "the American nightmare," which all African descendants growing up in the United States face, should not be minimized; still, it is important to expand the concept of racism to encompass other racial groups that face similar racist structures. For, in the mind of the white center, "colored" refers to anyone who is not white, that is, from European stock.

While African Americans served as slaves in the antebellum South, Amerindians faced systematic genocide throughout the West, and Latino/as were brutalized throughout the Southwest. Asians also experienced everything from murder while the transcontinental railroad was being built (so as to avoid paying them wages) to concentration camps in the early 1940s during the Second World War. And Jews were always viewed with suspicion, at times becoming the targets of hate crimes and mob violence. Any discussion of racism must move beyond a black-and-white dichotomy to explore how the Bible has been read to justify the oppression of these historically oppressed groups within the United States.

African Americans

According to the U.S. Constitution, written in 1787, in determining political representation, nonwhites were to be counted as three-fifths of a person (Art. 1, Sec. 2.3). Legal, economic, and political mechanisms were established by the young republic to maintain a viable institution, even though many people of African descent gave their lives fighting for liberty in the Revolutionary War. Normalizing slavery as an institution also required some sort of religious legitimation. The men who penned the Constitution also held the power to make their worldview, including their reading of the Bible, normative for the entire fledgling nation.

Biblical interpretations are dependent on who is doing the reading and the interpreting. For the dominant culture, as we have seen in the first chapter, black is defined as impure, a definition that "colors" how the Bible is read. This definition influences how Euroamericans interpret the role of blacks in the Bible. If black is equated with sin, then the Bible is read in a way that promotes this presupposition. For example, some still maintain that the mark of Cain was blackness. Cain, you will recall, slew his brother Abel out of jealousy. When confronted by God, Cain feared that others would take vengeance for his deed. In an effort to protect Cain from being killed, the Bible states that God placed a mark upon him. According to Genesis: "And Yahweh set a mark on Cain so that anyone who found him should not kill him" (4:15). Historically, the mark of Cain was understood as God making Cain black.

Similarly, the curse of Ham was also interpreted as blackness. After the flood, Ham gazed upon his father Noah's nakedness while Noah was in a drunken stupor. According to Genesis, when Noah awoke and discovered what Ham had done, he said of Ham's son, "Cursed be Canaan; he shall be a slave of slaves to his brothers" (9:25). Interpreters and scholars again attached blackness to the curse even though, in the case of both Cain and Canaan, no mention was made of their skin color. The mark or curse placed upon them could easily have been whiteness. However, because the dominant culture has defined blackness as evil and whiteness as pure, it only made sense to attach blackness to Cain's mark and Ham's curse.

During the Age of Exploration in the 1500s, white Christians began in earnest to profit from the slave trade. The transoceanic journey, known as the Middle Passage, represents the largest migration (forced or voluntary) in modern history, with estimates somewhere between nine and fifty million Africans over a four-century period. These Africans were needed to tame the land of the so-called New World, but first they had to be tamed. The domestication of Africans could not occur until the center was theologically able to justify this form of oppression. One response was to advocate the existence of pre-Adam races. Blacks, like the beasts of the fields, were created prior to Adam.[2] This also helps explain from where Cain's wife came. If there were only two people in the world, Adam and Eve, and they had two sons, Cain and Abel, where did Cain's future wife or, for that matter, the village mentioned in Genesis 4:17 come from? Thus, it was theorized that this village was composed of blacks, a pre-Adam race, a type of subhuman classification.

This raised interesting theological questions. Did blacks have souls? Could they be saved? Did they have the capacity for salvation? Some slaveholders viewed Africans to be like other farm animals, which were capital commodities and did not have souls, while more liberal-minded slaveholders maintained that blacks might have souls but were simply too brutish to undergo Christian instruction or catechism. Either way, slaveholders required total authority and unlimited power, including the right to mutilate slaves by detaching limbs needed for escape, to physically torture slaves, as in whippings, eye gouging, tongue slitting, branding, and castration, depending on the slave's "offense," and to kill slaves with impunity. These rights insured a social order that secured the position of whites within society.

In the early 1700s laws were passed throughout the colonies forbidding the baptism of slaves lest their freedom in Christ be interpreted other than spiritually. Many slaveholders feared Christianity would lead slaves to the dangerous conclusion that they had dignity due to Christ's salvific act, making them "uppity" if not downright rebellious. Evangelists interested in reaching the slave population for Christ first had to assure the slaveholders that the conversion of their "livestock" was in their best interest because it would create more obedient and humble slaves who would now labor for the master as for Christ. When it was determined that slaves were somewhat worthy of salvation, the institution of slavery turned into a means by which the gospel could be spread, and thus became justifiable.

White Christians were able to support slavery because it provided the "heathen" Africans an opportunity to hear the gospel and obtain eternal life. Their salvation (the spiritual) took precedence over their physical bondage (the material). To the Eurocentric mind-set, salvation was not the only benefit slave-bound Africans received. Additionally, they were taught civilization, how to distinguish good from evil, and basic reasoning abilities that elevated them from the "bestial sloth" of their existence. Slavery was as beneficial to the Africans as to the Euroamerican masters who were charged with their tutelage—if not more so.

The Great Awakening, a pietistic movement that emphasized the need for a personal experience of conversion, swept throughout the colonies in the mid-1730s. This religious phenomenon served as a watershed for the conversion of many to Christianity, including Africans. Nevertheless, the motif of liberation found in the Bible had to be reconciled with the slaveholders' desire to convert their property into obedient Christians. Slaves could be Christianized as long as it was recognized that the New Testament did not speak out against slavery; hence, Old Testament references to slavery remained authoritative. If Jesus Christ would have considered slavery to be a sin, surely he would have directly said so.

Consequently, slaves were cautiously proselyted.[3] In spite of slave-holders' attempts to ignore the liberative motif of the Gospels, some slaves were radicalized by the victory of the resurrection of Christ, and many took up arms against their oppressors as a Christian action to gain a physical liberation that would match their spiritual freedom.

Blacks were at all costs discouraged from reading the Bible lest they equate liberation in Christ with liberation in the world. Hence, white society, specifically Protestant white society, found itself censoring the Bible by determining what its slave population could and could not hear. Crucial to the maintenance of the American slavocracy was the overall systematic prohibition for blacks, slaves, and free Africans to learn how to read the Bible, or any other book for that matter. Laws forbade anyone from providing scholastic instruction to African slaves, and the general teaching of freed slaves was discouraged. Such restrictions prevented those of African descent from exploring the world outside their confined social location and made them dependent on white society to define and interpret reality for them, a reality that included the Bible.

The norm of keeping African Americans uneducated continued for a century after legislation ended slavery. It was not until the 1954 Supreme Court decision *Brown v. Topeka Board of Education* that the purpose of segregation was unmasked and the right of African Americans to education was established, a right that has yet to be fulfilled half a century later. The response of most white churches to the "threat" of integration is worth noting. Many Christian schools (K through 12) were established by churches during this era of public-school desegregation. The dominant culture's Christian response was often to provide an alternative to desegregation, masked under the cloak of providing a "Christian" education.

Because the master controlled what portions of the Bible would be taught to slaves, most of the biblical stories and teachings selected attempted to justify the master's self-interest. Most sermons were based on passages like Ephesians 6:5, which states, "Slaves, obey your masters according to the flesh, with fear and trembling, and in singleness of heart, as unto Christ." The interpretation from the center of slavocracy urged slaves to fulfill God's will by being docile and obedient so that they could be blessed by God with eternal salvation.

Yet, whenever the Bible is used to justify oppression, the margins read the Bible to understand their oppression and to seek their liberation. While white preachers in the employ of the masters interpreted the biblical stories spiritually and metaphorically, black slaves interpreted these same stories materially and literally (i.e., God's liberation of the Hebrew slaves in Egypt was a physical, not just a spiritual, liberation). Such readings reserved the right to resist passages within the text that had been historically used by the dominant culture to justify the dehumanization of oppressed groups. For this reason, one would be hard pressed even today to find sermons within the African American community based on Philemon (where Paul sends a runaway slave back to his master) or to hear any Negro spirituals honoring Paul, who penned passages such as Ephesians 6:5.

Yet the picking and choosing of which Scriptures to obey and which to ignore becomes problematic for the person of faith who looks to the Bible for guidance. How are apparent contradictions in the text to be interpreted? For example, the biblical text warns believers to obey governments. The letter to the Romans states, "Let every soul be subject to higher authorities. For there is no authority except from God, but the authorities which exist are ordained by God" (13:1). Yet, in the book of Acts, this same Bible states that when Peter and the other apostles were brought before the political authorities for disobeying the decree to remain silent about Christ Jesus, they answered by saying, "It is right to obey God rather than men" (5:29). Which of these two conflicting Scriptures should be the basis for Christian political action? Both, depending on the contexts from which the Bible is read. For example, when antebellum Northerners, in obedience to Romans 13:1, returned runaway slaves to their Southern masters, they acted against the gospel message of Jesus about bringing "abundant life," as crystalized in John 10:10. Their actions instead brought death. In similar fashion, African Americans who read the biblical text from the historical context of slavery, which based its moral justification on selective writings of Paul, now reject the passages that were used to rob their collective existence of dignity.[4]

Amerindians

The Exodus story of God's chosen people being led by the Almighty to the promised land and taking possession of it has become a fundamental model for most liberative readings of the Bible. Yet the question that seems to be ignored is what happened to the Canaanites who were already in possession of the land. How can we reconcile God the merciful with God the conqueror? How do we come to understand passages like Deuteronomy 7:1–2, which states,

> When Yahweh your God brings you into the land which you are going to possess, and he casts out many nations from before you, the Hittites, the Girgashites, the Amorites, the Canaanites, the Perizzites, the Hivites, and the Jebusites, seven nations larger and mightier than you; and when Yahweh your God gives them up before you, you are to strike them, you shall utterly destroy them, you shall not make a covenant with them, nor show mercy to them.

Even children and infants were to be slaughtered. Is God calling for genocide? How do we come to understand passages like Joshua 6:21? "And [the Hebrews] destroyed all that was in the city [of Jericho] from man even to woman, from young even to the aged, and even the ox, and sheep, and ass, by the edge of the sword." This slaughter of all humans (including children) and animal life became the acceptable pattern of holy war as the Hebrews conquered the occupied territories.[5] How can the God of love order such massacres? More succinctly, how can this new God of the invading oppressors become the liberator of those whose death is required?

Centuries after the slaughter of the Canaanites in the book of Joshua, King David used these passages to legitimate the subjugation of the Canaanites living during his reign. Millenniums later, these same stories were used by Europeans to justify the possession of their promised land, the Americas, and the extermination of the new Canaanites, whom they called Indians. Since the beginning of the conquest of South America, Amerindians were considered to be soulless subhumans, a view that exonerated the conquistadors from any spiritual responsibility for their souls. A complex, lively discussion developed at the University of Salamanca in Spain over the condition of the Amerindians' souls, the right to enslave them, and the right to take their land. The humanity and capacity for salvation of the Amerindians were not proclaimed until 1537 when the bull *Sublimis Deus* was issued by Pope Paul III.[6] The bull refuted the conquistador construction of the Amerindians as soulless humans or talking animals. Meanwhile, in North America, the construction of Amerindians as savages needing eradication was fully developed along spiritual lines. Making their intentions known, Christian preachers often referred to these Amerindians as *Canaanites,* in need of conversion or annihilation. Amerindians, in the eyes of the dominant culture, were pagan savages needing to be civilized and Christianized. Because of the consequences of conquest, many Amerindians found solidarity with the original indigenous population of the promised land, thus leading them to read the Exodus story with Canaanite eyes.

The Hebrew's (European's) dream of religious freedom and liberation became the Canaanite's (Amerindian's) nightmare of subjugation and genocide. Like the Canaanites before them, the Amerindians were viewed as a people who could not be trusted, a snare to the righteous, and a culture that required decimation. Reading the Bible through "Canaanite" eyes has led Amerindian theologians (as well as present-day Palestinian theologians) to question the Exodus story as an appropriate biblical model for understanding their own struggle for dignity. They call for Christian reflection that places the Canaanites at the center of theological thought and that considers the violence and injustice rarely mentioned in critical works concerning Exodus. To read with Canaanite eyes insures that the entire Bible will be read, not just the passages that inspire conquest or justify genocide.[7]

So, can the Bible be read with Canaanite eyes? Some Amerindians believe that it can. In chapter 1 we reviewed the story of the Canaanite woman who came to Jesus asking for healing for her daughter. Matthew 15:21–28 records Jesus telling this Canaanite woman, "I was sent only to the lost sheep of the house of Israel. It is not good to take the bread of the children and throw it to the dogs." The Canaanite woman, a descendent of the original people who occupied the land before it became promised, faced the full rejection of the same God who called for her people's death. Nevertheless, in this passage, the Canaanites became the center of theological thought. The Canaanite woman of old, like Amerindians of today, challenged Jesus' exclusive understanding of the gospel, liberating him from a social location responsible for constructing racist stereotypes. The miracle of the story goes beyond the healing of her "pagan" daughter; rather, Jesus' own heart and mind were transformed as he recognized the inclusive essence of the gospel that embraces Canaanites and Amerindians alike.[8]

Asians

Most African American, feminist, and Hispanic Christian communities are situated in a dominant culture that primarily professes Christianity. Asians, however, have their roots in a continent where interreligious dialogues are important because Christianity is a tiny minority where only 3 percent of the population identify themselves as Christians. Christianity has an "outsider" status because of its limited effect on Asian culture, whose symbols, expressions, worldview, and language are unfamiliar to a Western mind-set. Additionally, Christianity was often linked in the minds of many people of Asia (and Africa) with Western domination and was seen as a product of Western colonialism. Missionaries often introduced the Bible to people whom they considered to be culturally inferior and ensnared in idolatry, superstition, and heathen worship. An old African proverb says it best: "At first the Europeans had the Bible and we had the land; now the Europeans have the land and we have the Bible." It is important to maintain a global perspective: two-thirds of the world is non-Christian, existing mainly under the yoke of economic exploitation by the one-third of the world associated with the Christian community. Reading the Bible, then, goes beyond spiritual interpretation alone.

For Christianity to survive in Asia, it has to coexist with other religious traditions. This social location has also led the Asian American faith community to understand the Bible through a hermeneutic in which all sacred books from different religious traditions are allowed to participate in the religious dialogue and contribute from the wisdom literature of their different Asian cultures. Until now, biblical truth was created from the social location of Western scholars, missionaries, and clerics who reserved for themselves the sole authority for determining how the Bible was to be interpreted. This right of the West to claim a preferential option in interpreting Scripture has been generally rejected by those who have been colonialized.

To the Asian or Asian American Christian, Western Christianity is seen as a captive of Greek philosophy, Roman structures, and the Latin language. How then can Western Christians rediscover and richly enhance their faith? Some Asian Christians have suggested using a "third-eye" theology. To open a "third eye," according to Japanese Zen master Daisetz Suzuki, is a Buddhist call to become open to that which is unnoticed due to one's own ignorance. As ignorance dissipates, the infinity of heaven is manifested as we learn to see ourselves with this new eye. To read with a third eye allows Christianity to turn to the abundant indigenous stories, legends, and folklore of the people. To the missionaries, these stories were pagan, if not satanic, and so they were suppressed and banned. Nevertheless, Asian Christians are reclaiming them, stories from the underside of world history, to serve as the most authentic symbols by which they can understand the Bible.

Through storytelling, Asian communities are able to liberate themselves from the restrictive interpretations of the missionaries, who represented the Eurocentric understanding of the Bible and inhibited the flourishing of Asian humanity. Asians are enhancing their theological understanding of how God saves inside and outside Western Christian history and discovering, through ancient Asian wisdom, deeper truths about God and humanity's sufferings and hardships. Through such indigenous stories, transmitted from generation to generation, consciousness is raised about the power of love, humanity, justice, and morality. These stories lead to communion within the human community and with God. Furthermore, these stories illustrate spiritual dimensions found within the Bible, making biblical texts accessible to cultures that view Westerners suspiciously. In the tradition of Jesus, who also spoke in stories about the divine (parables), Asian communities reach deep into their rich heritage to provide the lens by which the Bible can be understood and interpreted.[9]

To read the Bible from an Asian perspective is to also read from a postcolonialist context, cognizant of how Western imperialist powers used the Scriptures to impose a Western dominance over other lands and people. Instrumental in the conquest of the two-thirds world by the European center was a biblical reading that cloaked its true intentions with religious sensibilities. This venture was successful because it usually left the indigenous population susceptible to conquest by wreaking havoc on its self-understanding and worldview. For example, in the missionary zeal to eliminate idols, evangelists engaged in a crusade to topple powerful religious symbols. This was the case with the practice of Chinese ancestor worship, which was understood by the missionaries as idolatrous. Missionaries interpreted 1 Corinthians 8:4–6 to prohibit the offering of food to ancestors, a common practice among Chinese communities, as well as other Asian communities. Seeing the societal practice of making offerings to ancestors as a form of idolatry, they ignored the social context that gave rise to this tradition among the Chinese.

According to Confucius, the greatest virtue is filial piety, the first principle of heaven, the ultimate standard by which people are to conduct their lives. In a time of societal breakdown, marked by intellectual dogma, moral uncertainties, and political instability, Confucius turned to *hsiao* ("filial piety") as a way of restoring harmony and promoting family values. *Hsiao* encourages family reunions at ancestral shrines and support to bereaved family members both financially and emotionally. In effect, *hsiao* is a deep-rooted expression of devotion that reaffirms the basic understandings of family duty, obligation, values, and responsibility. Most who participate in *hsiao* are not seeking blessings, protection, or guidance from the deceased through some form of supernatural power; rather, they are connecting earthly care for family elders with their spiritual well-being. A distinction is made between worshiping ancestors as deities and a ritual that links the living presence of the dead with the consciousness of the bereaved. For Western Christians to declare this social practice idolatrous and prohibit it upon conversion to Christianity is tantamount to advising the Chinese not to love their elder parents or demonstrate that love by caring for them. In short, not to be Chinese![10]

Jews

"The Jews killed our Lord and Savior Jesus Christ, and for this, they must be punished." This understanding of present-day Judaism is based on a misreading of Matthew 27:25. According to the text, Pilate, a Gentile, was willing to let Jesus go, but the Jewish crowd insisted that Jesus be crucified. When Pilate claimed that he would be innocent of Jesus' blood, the crowd responded, "The blood [of Jesus] will be on us and on our children." The passage has historically been interpreted by the Christian church as the self-imposed curse of Jews for their supposed role in the crucifixion of Jesus. Gentiles are held blameless through the act of Pontius Pilate "washing his hands" of the blood of Jesus.

Besides, for many Christians, Jews stubbornly rejected numerous passages in the Hebrew Bible that foretold the coming of the Messiah. In the minds of a dominant culture, where Christians are God's chosen people, something suspicious exists in the "perverse" act of a people clinging to an ancient religion "proven false" by the coming of Christ.

Yet, the roots of anti-Semitism go deeper than simply a Jewish versus Christian understanding of Jesus. During the early development of Christianity, specifically during the medieval period, Christians interpreted Exodus 22:25 literally: "If you lend silver to my people, the poor among you, you shall not be as a moneylender, you shall not charge usury." For a Christian to charge interest meant he or she could be excommunicated or killed by the church. Even to discuss the possibility of charging interest on a loan was sufficient grounds for burning a theologian at the stake. Jews, however, rejected the Christian interpretation of this passage, basing their understanding on Deuteronomy: "You may lend to a stranger at interest, but not to your brother, so that Yahweh your God may bless you in all that you put your hand to in the land where you go to possess" (23:21).

Free to lend money and charge interest, many Jewish businessmen found a niche within Christian society. Jewish families were left to handle banking transactions, an important need for the development of Christian Europe. Ironically, several Jewish families found themselves financing many Christian advances toward domination, specifically the numerous Crusades. But what can be thought of a group of people who prospered at a trade that good God-fearing Christians believed contradicted the Bible? As Christians throughout Europe prepared to march in order to liberate Jerusalem from the infidels, often the would-be crusaders realized the paradox of riding to fight God's enemies in Palestine when God's greater enemies, the crucifiers of Jesus, remained in European cities to prosper. And this was also viewed by some as a great opportunity to eliminate the moneylenders to whom large sums of funds were owed. "Kill the Jews" became a Christian battle cry throughout Europe, a cry heard as recently as the 1940s.

Even though Christians eventually reinterpreted the Bible so that they too could charge interest, the stereotype of Jews as money mongers continued to develop. This would give rise to the anti-Semitic belief that Jews controlled the world's financial institutions as well as the media and every conceivable left-leaning organization. The *Polemical Protocols of the Elders of Zion,* which made its appearance at the turn of the twentieth century, supposedly was documented proof that an international Jewish conspiracy existed. Believers in this international Jewish conspiracy have turned to the Bible to find justification for their views of Jews, whom they believe are unsaved due to their rejection of Jesus as the Messiah. Jews then became the children of darkness, followers of the Antichrist, and as such should be contained if not eliminated. Yet such interpreters of the Bible seem to forget that Y'shua was the name by which Jesus was known during his earthly ministry and the man called John the Baptist was known by his contemporaries as Yochanan ben Zechariah. The individuals responsible for the development of what we today call Christianity were Jews. In its truest sense, Christianity is not a religion apart from Judaism but rather a branch grafted onto the vine of Judaism and thus deeply rooted in the Jewish faith.

Paul argues that the Gentiles are grafted onto the Jewish olive tree so that the "rich sap" that flows from its holy roots can reach the pagans (Rom. 11:16–24). Even though Paul struggles with the segments of the Jewish community that rejected Jesus' messiahship, he does not condemn the Jews. Quite the contrary, although upset with their rejection of Jesus, he still affirms their place as "God's chosen people, still beloved by God" (Rom. 11:28). Paul makes it clear that their inheritance in God's reign is still valid, "for the free gifts and choices of God are irrevocable" (Rom. 11:29).

JUSTIFYING CLASSISM

Every day, along with most adult Americans, I must receive about half a dozen offers for credit cards. It seems as if every bank in the

United States wants to provide me with cash at an introductory offer of 3 percent or less. One specific advertisement caught my eye. It boldly proclaimed,

> Switch to the one credit card that helps spread the Gospel of Christ. . . . At last—a MasterCard that shares the love of Christ. As a Christian, why would you use any other card?

Here is how the card works: every time a purchase is made, a contribution is made, at no cost to the cardholder, to WXHL, a Christian radio station in the Philadelphia region. Fulfilling the capitalist dream of buying on credit for items that I cannot afford and probably do not need has never been easier. The guilt associated with conspicuous consumption is now offset by my commitment to spreading the gospel. Flashing my plastic card, with the dove and cross on it, becomes a witness to the sales clerk of my commitment to Christ! This credit card demonstrates how our society has merged our present economic system with the way the dominant culture does church.

Of course, churches need not stop with credit cards. In an era of marketing to increase production (church membership and saved souls), churches are opening Starbucks outlets in their fellowship halls as well as other food court–type restaurants, like McDonalds, complete with drive-through windows. Other churches have transformed their sanctuaries into health clubs, complete with indoor Olympic-size pools, racketball courts, running tracks, and basketball courts. In some churches, for a slight fee of about $300, you can obtain a membership to use the house of God. Many churches, as a testimony to God's blessings, are constructing cathedrals with memberships in the tens of thousands and operating budgets that rival many relief organizations set up to deal with the physical needs of the world's disenfranchised. At times these megachurches, mostly located in middle-class suburbia, contrast with the misery in the urban centers of this nation, where, in most cases, the wealth of these churchgoers is created.

Many churches mirror the conspicuous consumption of the overall culture. Bigger and newer is better as churches begin to resemble shopping malls with multiple outlets for their parishioners/customers. In certain areas, belonging to a particular church indicates one's socioeconomic level, enhancing possible business and political contacts.

Economic philosophers like Thorstein Veblen (1857–1929) critique the typical consumer who acquires goods that do not satisfy any particular need. Such conspicuous consumption of a commodity is usually undertaken to enhance the reputation of the consumer. The flaunting of "luxury" commodities causes an "invidious comparison" to occur among those consumers who are unable to obtain this particular commodity.[11] Examples include placing undue emphasis on the clothing labels we wear, the car we drive, the neighborhood we live in, and, yes, the church we attend. Certain churches propagate the view that those who belong to their congregations are closer to biblical accuracy and truth than other churches, specifically those of other denominations. The success of the church (measured by growth) serves as proof of God's approval. Success in ministry is demonstrated by God's blessings, in the form of a bigger sanctuary, a larger congregation, or greater community recognition.

When was the connection made between economic success and God's blessings? For sociologist Max Weber (1864–1920), the exchange between a religion that encouraged an ethics of abstinence (understood as puritanism) and economic success within modern social life (or, as he calls it, the spirit of capitalism) can be traced to the theology of John Calvin (1509–1564). Weber's understanding of Calvin led him to contend that Protestantism, as a religious ideology, was able to dismantle inhibiting factors of Catholicism that prevented the development of a modern economic system. By spiritualizing the very nature of capitalism, Weber concluded that capitalism was able to flourish in Europe because it provided a rational response to the religious teachings concerning the "Protestant work ethic."

According to Calvin's monumental work, *Institutes of the Christian Religion*, God determines the eternal fate of each person. Those who are elected are chosen not because of anything they may have done but purely by the grace and mercy of God. God knows who is elected, but how do the elect know they are chosen? After all, according to Calvin, they cannot rely on feeling (as in the case of a conversion experience) because feelings are deceptive.

Nor can they rely on good works, because salvation is a gift, not something earned. Nor does church membership assure salvation, for there are those who attend churches that are not chosen (i.e., the Catholic Church, according to Calvin).

According to Weber, one knew that one was saved by the visible fruits produced by one's labor. Weber understood Calvinism in a way that linked capitalism with Protestantism. God requires Christians to attain social achievements because it is the will of God that social life be organized according to God's commandments and purpose. Labor ceases to be mundane as it is elevated to the realm of a divine calling, a proposition also voiced by Martin Luther. God predestines not only eternal salvation and damnation but also one's occupation. If the only purpose of the elect is to glorify God by fulfilling God's will and purpose, then labor becomes one means by which the elect can promote the glory of God. As Protestantism, specifically Calvinism, developed, one's faith was provable in worldly activities.

The process of sanctifying life took on the character of a business enterprise as the followers of Calvin saw the undeniable proof of being chosen by God in financial success. God blessed the trade of God's chosen. One was to work hard, cognizant that a wasted hour of work was an hour lost to labor for God's glory. Not working became tantamount to lacking God's salvific grace. In fact, if God provided a way to lawfully and ethically create more wealth and a person refused this new calling, the person was refusing to be God's steward. A spiritual duty existed to labor and become rich, not for the flesh but for God. What Jesus condemned as service to mammon became acceptable if mammon was pursued for the glory of God.[12]

Yet, if wealth indicates closeness to God, does poverty mean God's rejection? Is the unequal distribution of resources in this world a special divine dispensation, which, like grace, is distributed according to God's will? Not only do I have a right to my riches as a blessing of God for my faithfulness in glorifying God through my labor; the poverty of others is not connected to my riches but is the will of God! Even if the impoverished are poorly paid, they are to work to the glory of God, for this is what pleases God. In effect, this legitimizes the exploitation of workers by making the capitalist business not a venture for profit but a calling from God.

From the center of economic power, the Bible is read with the assumption that riches are a blessing or, at the very least, are good; hence, references to riches must be read in a positive manner. When a passage seems to condemn riches or the wealthy, it is read metaphorically so that the text can mean something else. The reader imposes upon the literal text a framework that adds attitudes, intentions, or motivation.[13] Thus, when Luke 4:19 says the gospel is for the poor, we interpret it to mean poor in spirit, thus moving from a literal meaning that connects the text to the perspective of the poor toward a spiritualized devotional interpretation that collapses any differences between the poor and rich, the oppressed and their oppressors. When the Bible is read from a middle- and upper-class social location, that reading becomes normative for the entire society because those who benefit from concentrated wealth have the aggregated power to shape a "legitimate" rendering of the biblical text. Such a reading condones what Jesus condemns, rendering impotent his radical pronouncements on economic relationships.

Because anyone can "make it" in this country, those who fail (live in poverty) have no one to blame but themselves. And worst, we associate their lack of blessings in labor to be a clear sign of God's rejection of them. The emphasis, then, is placed upon saving souls. If the person in poverty is first saved, then God's blessings will follow. Missing from the discourse is how poverty is caused—specifically, how through classism a certain segment of the population must be kept poor so that the dominant culture can benefit and maintain its level of luxury.

A functional analysis of poverty shows that, in most cases, the wealth of the rich is directly related to the poverty of the poor. First, poverty ensures that a segment of the population (which coincidently is mainly composed of people of color) does the undesirable work of the society, work that is physically dangerous or dirty. They occupy menial, dead-end, underpaid jobs. A low-wage labor pool provides unprecedented profits for different industries, such as agriculture and segments of the garment industry, whose profits are dependent on the economic exploitation of the poor. Second, the low wages paid to those who are poor subsidize middle- and upper-class lifestyles. This includes cheap labor in the form of domestic help, such as nannies, gardeners, and maids, who provide the affluent with free time to participate in more enriching activities—social clubs, parties, and charity events. Additionally, because those who are poor pay a higher proportion of income and property taxes, they also subsidize local and state government services that are geared to benefit more affluent groups. Third, poverty creates jobs—not just dysfunctional jobs like drug dealing, the production and sale of cheap liquor, pawn shops, and prostitution—but respectable professional jobs in penology, criminology, public-health work, social work, and the social sciences. Fourth, the poor extend the economic usefulness of goods by buying what others do not want, including expired food items, secondhand clothes, and run-down houses and automobiles. Poverty also provides numerous social and physiological benefits to the affluent, including, but not limited to, the self-construction of the wealthy as hard workers who earned their riches, a permanent measuring rod for status, an object for the benevolence of the wealthy, and a group to blame for the downward mobility of the middle class, victims of an ever-expanding income gap.[14]

In a world that contains about 6 billion people, the World Bank estimates that 1.3 billion live in dire poverty while another 2 billion simply live in poverty. More than 3 billion people, the majority of the world, live on less than two dollars a day. According to the United Nations, 1.45 billion people lack health services, 1.33 billion lack safe drinking water, and 2.25 billion lack proper sanitation, crucial needs when we consider that children are 60 percent less likely to die when these services are provided. Each year 17 million people die from preventable parasitic diseases caused mainly by a lack of these services.

The poorest 60 percent of the world's population own only 6 percent of the world's wealth, and the richest 20 percent own 85 percent of the world's income, producing 66 percent of the world's greenhouse gasses and consuming 70 percent of the world's energy, 75 percent of the world's metals, and 85 percent of the world's wood. Yet we blame the strain in world resources on overpopulated areas like China or India. In reality, the 50 million people that will be added to the U.S. population over the next forty years will have the equivalent global impact (in terms of the consumption of the world's resources) of an additional 2 billion people in India.[15] The world's rich minority, which controls a monopoly on the vast majority of the world's resources, is in need of liberation from the sin of hoarding. Reading the Bible from the margins is as concerned with the liberation of the vast majority of the world's population that lives in misery as it is with the salvation of the world's minority that lives in privilege.

Five percent of the U.S. population gather around their tables and eat to their hearts' content. The scraps they leave behind are more than what many of the world's inhabitants will eat that day. Yet the Gospel of Luke records Jesus saying,

> When you make dinner or supper, do not call your friends, nor your siblings, nor your relatives, nor your rich neighbors, lest they invite you in return and it becomes a repayment to you. But when you have a party, invite the poor, the maimed, the lame, and the blind, and you will be blessed, for they cannot repay you. (14:12–14)

Classism from the Margins

Have you ever read a Gospel parable, only to think how unfair it was? For example, in Matthew 20:1–16 Jesus tells the story of a vineyard owner who early in the morning sets out to hire laborers. He goes to the local gathering place where laborers usually wait to be hired, negotiates a fair day's wages (a denarius), and sends them to his fields. Several hours later, mid-morning, he comes across some individuals who have yet to be hired, so he employs them and sends them to his fields. At noon, he finds more unemployed laborers and sends them to his fields. This process is again repeated in the mid- and late afternoon. When the day ends and it is time to pay the workers, the vineyard owner reverses the order and begins to pay those who were hired last and only worked a few hours. He begins by paying them the same amount he originally agreed to pay those first hired. When it is time to pay those who worked the entire day, he pays the same amount of money as those who only worked a few hours. Some worked all day, some just a few hours, yet everyone got the same amount of money. Now, is this fair? Is it any wonder that those who worked all day grumbled against the vineyard owner? Shouldn't workers be paid according to the amount of time they invested in the job?

In order to reconcile how fairness is defined on the basis of our present capitalist economic system and how the biblical passage defines fairness, the Bible must be read metaphorically. Then the parable is understood as God providing the gift of salvation (the denarius) without regard to how much work is done by the individual or how long one has labored for God. All who come to God are given the same portion of grace regardless of when in their life journey they turned to God. While such a spiritual reading may provide additional insight, to read the text solely metaphorically and avoid a material reading allows the reader to justify the injustices of the present economic system and ignore the radical call of being a disciple of Jesus.

For those who are undocumented and accustomed to stand at designated street corners throughout major cities of this country, waiting and hoping for a patron to stop and offer a job (off the books to avoid employment taxes), the fairness of this parable resonates. For those who are relegated to the ghettos and *barrios*, unemployed or limited to minimum-wage service jobs, the fairness of this parable provides a vision for a just society based on the rule of God. How many of these migrant workers end up working all day, only to be paid a fraction of their worth because they are undocumented? How many times has the employer contacted the INS to show up at the end of the workday to arrest the "illegals" and get out of paying them for their work? Or how many of these workers injure themselves at the job, only to be dropped off at the closest hospital and left to fend for themselves? To read this parable from the margins, from the perspective of the poor, is to recognize that the vineyard owner, that is, the employer, has a responsibility toward the laborers, a responsibility that goes beyond what traditional capitalist thinking defines as just.

To read the text materially is to realize Jesus' awareness of the laborer's plight. Poverty is usually defined as a lack of resources, specifically money. Yet poverty's dysfunctions encompass a higher likelihood of failed marriages; a higher susceptibility to illness, disease, and sickness; a greater likelihood of having children who will not complete high school; a higher probability of having children who will have difficulties with law enforcement agencies; a greater chance of being a victim of a crime; and a shorter life expectancy. Poverty can never be defined simply as a lack of money; it is a debilitating lifestyle that robs its victim of dignity and personhood.

Jesus fully understood that poverty prevented those who were created in the image of God from participating in the abundant life he came to give. In his parable of the Vineyard Owner, Jesus attempts to teach economic justice so that all can have life abundantly. He recognized that it was not the laborers' fault that they failed to obtain employment for that day. They awoke in the early predawn, walked to the spot where potential employers came to find workers, and waited. Regardless of whether they were chosen to work or not, they still needed a denarius to meet their basic needs: food, shelter, clothing. To be chosen to work for only half a day and to be paid half a denarius was insufficient. Half a denarius meant that several family members would not eat that day. Only an uncaring and unmerciful heart will declare it just that these laborers leave without being able to meet their basic needs because, through no fault of their own, they were unable to find a job. The biblical teaching is that those who are economically privileged, like the vineyard owner, must remain responsible for those who are not.

As important as the metaphorical rendering of the parable of the Vineyard Owner may be, just as important, if not more so, is the material reading. For those living under an economic system that commodifies time, justice is defined as a set pay for a set number of hours worked. However, Jesus defines justice as insuring that each worker obtains a living wage, regardless of the hours worked, so that all can share in the abundant life. It did not matter how many hours a laborer worked; what mattered was that, at the end of the day, she or he took home a living wage so that the entire family could survive for another day. It was the worker's responsibility to labor; it was the employer's responsibility that the employee left work with enough. What does this say about our present system, where, if a person works full-time at the minimum hourly wage, he or she will earn several thousand dollars below what the U.S. government has determined to be the poverty level?

Simply stated, the Scriptures have little patience with those who are rich and ignore the plight of the poor, even when the rich are not necessarily responsible for the poverty. Examine another parable, the one about Lazarus and the rich man. According to Luke 16:19–31, there once lived a man of great wealth who feasted only on the best each day. At the gate of his mansion lay a poor man called Lazarus, who was covered with sores and dreamed of the day he could dine on the scraps that fell from the rich man's table. Both men died. Lazarus was carried by angels to the bosom of Abraham, but the rich man was sent to hell to be tormented. The rich man, seeing Lazarus in Abraham's bosom, pleaded for mercy. He asked to have a few drops of water placed on his tongue to cool the agony of the flames. Abraham refused because of the great gulf separating heaven from hell. The rich man then asked to have Lazarus go back to his family to warn them of the danger of their riches. This too was denied, for, as Abraham stated, "if they were not willing to hear Moses and the prophets, even if one from the dead should rise, they will not be persuaded."

Nowhere in the text does it tell us that the rich man's wealth was accumulated unjustly or that he was directly oppressing Lazarus. His judgment and condemnation to hell were based solely on the fact that he was rich and failed to share his resources with those, like Lazarus, who lacked the basics for survival. In this case, God's judgment was not based on anything the rich man did or any belief system he confessed; rather, it was based on what he failed to do. He failed to use his resources so that others could also enjoy an abundant life. Mary's Magnificat, found in Luke, is fulfilled: "[God] pulled down potentates from their thrones and exalted the humble. God filled the hungry with good things and sent the rich away empty" (1:52–53). Why? As Proverbs states, "The one oppressing the poor curses their Creator, but the one honoring God has mercy on the needy" (14:31). One's relationship with the poor is linked to one's relationship with God, a concept that will be explored in greater detail in chapter 6, above.

The Bible does not call for the giving of our spare change to the poor; rather, it calls for a radical restructuring of our economic structures, which privilege 5 percent of the world's population with the greatest wealth and riches ever known to humanity while the vast majority of the world struggles for its daily bread. Vast economic differences in the distribution of wealth create structural injustice, where the wealthy continue to enrich themselves and the poor sink into greater want. Present extremes in wealth and poverty contradict the very nature of the Year of Jubilee as explained in Leviticus 25 and Deuteronomy 15. Simply stated, the Bible required that all lands be returned to their original owners every fifty years and all debts be forgiven every seven years.

Under such a system, the rich never became exceedingly rich nor the poor exceedingly poor. Every fifty years, the Bible required a redistribution of resources to prevent the hoarding of goods.

In his 1776 book *The Wealth of Nations,* which has been foundational for the present U.S. economic system, Adam Smith concludes by exhorting the pursuit of economic self-interest, believing that an "invisible hand" will insure economic benefits for all of society within the context of unfettered supply and demand. Smith was confident that the enlightened self-interest of the capitalist would never lead the market economy to abuses like monopolies. Hence, no government had the right to interfere in the natural laws of supply and demand that determined the prices of goods, including wages. According to Smith, the pursuit of one's self-interest is good because it contributes to the overall common good. All have an absolute right, in fact a moral obligation, to follow their economic self-interest in order to fulfill their duty in creating a more just society. Free enterprise, economic individualism, and laissez-faire become the foundation of a just economic system and, for many Christians within the United States, a biblically based Christian economic system.

The apostle Paul, on the other hand, insists that Christians must constantly put the self-interest of others before themselves. In Ephesians he states, "Be subject to one another in the fear of the Lord" (5:21). In the Gospel of Matthew, Jesus is very direct:

> But it will not be so among you, but whoever among you would become great, let them be a servant to you. And whoever among you desires to be first, let them be a slave to you, for even the Son of Man did not come to be served, but to serve, and to give his life as a ransom for many. (20:26–27)

Jesus illustrated his willingness to deny his own self-interest by washing the feet of his disciples. To pursue self-interest is countered with becoming a servant to others. In fact, to pursue monetary self-interest, according to the biblical text, more than likely leads people away from God. In 1 Timothy, Paul warns,

> But those resolving to be rich fall into many foolish and hurtful lusts, a temptation and a snare which causes people to

sink into ruin and destruction. For the root of all evils is the love of money, having lusted after which some were seduced from the faith, and themselves pierced through by many pains. (6:9–10)

Christians reading the Bible through a metaphoric lens are quick to emphasize intention in this text. The *love* of money is what is condemned, not money itself. A material reading, however, insists that the action of pursuing riches is what ruins and destroys. The Bible's expectation of Christians is the complete opposite of what Smith advocates. Here is the question well-off Christians must answer: how do they reconcile Smith's claims of seeking self-interest, the foundation of a capitalist economy, with the biblical admonition to put the needs of others before one's own needs?

CHAPTER 4

Unmasking the Biblical
Justification of Sexism

As a field researcher conducting interviews in Patterson, New Jersey, during the mid-1990s, I was responsible for observing church life in predominantly poor congregations. Part of my task was to interview Latina/o church members, specifically Christians who attended a Pentecostal church. I remember a particular interview I conducted with an elderly woman, probably in her eighties. In many northeastern Pentecostal churches, women are very careful about the way they dress. In many cases, skirts come down to the ankle (even during the summer), and shirt tops are baggy so as to conceal the upper curves of the female body. I asked her why she dressed in this manner. Without much thought she quickly responded, "So as not to tempt the men." Frankly, I didn't have the heart to tell this eighty-year-old woman that she need not worry about this. Nevertheless, what I found fascinating about her comment was the way she saw herself—that is, through the eyes of the men of her church. Her activities, including the way she dressed her body, were molded by this viewpoint. From the pulpit, for all of her life, she has heard men preach about the sinful nature of women's bodies. It is the woman who leads men astray, and so she must be hidden from sight. Pious Christian women impose upon themselves their own subjugation by dressing the way men expect them to dress so that these same holy men do not fall into temptation. In my mind's eye I could just see her walking up to the female teenagers of the church to lecture them about their "improper" attire, thus maintaining a dress code established by

82

men and perpetuated by the church women, who have been taught to see themselves only through the eyes of men.

For many churches, any not biblically sanctioned sexual activity between men and women becomes the fault of the woman. How many times have you heard the same questions raised, at times by women, upon hearing of a rape? What was she wearing? What was she doing at that party? Why did she go out with those boys? How was she acting? Did she drink too much? What can you expect if she was asking for it? These questions, and many like them, underline a major component of patriarchy: women's bodies are evil and so lead righteous men to sin; hence the Bible grants authority to these holy men to protect and confine female bodies against sin. For the good of the community, for the purity of women, men must rule, a concept justified by how some men read the biblical text.

JUSTIFYING PATRIARCHY

At seminary I attended a class where the professor would begin each session by asking the students to call out their favorite biblical verse. This being a class full of future ministers and theologians, you can imagine the types of verses that were typically called out— John 3:16, Psalm 23, Romans 3:23, and Ephesians 2:8, to name a few. One day the professor looked in my direction and asked what was my favorite verse. Without hesitating I said Genesis 2:25, "And they were both naked, the man and his wife, yet they were not ashamed." I was not trying to be funny. I am attracted to this verse because I can find no better depiction of God's intention concerning human relationships, relationships where participants stand totally vulnerable before each other yet feel no shame. Nonetheless, the Bible is seen as patriarchal by many women who read the text.

Any examination of the biblical justification of patriarchy should begin with Genesis: "To the woman [God] said, 'I will greatly increase your sorrow in your childbearing; you shall bear children in sorrow, and your desire shall be for your husband, and he shall rule over you'" (3:16). Read through the eyes of patriarchy, the passage is quite straightforward. God has ordained men to rule over women. Historically, men have always cited the Bible to counteract women's attempts to advance in society. The Bible has been used to condemn female actions toward empowerment as unbiblical. In particular, many men have interpreted Genesis 3:16 to mean that because women first ate the mango (or apple) from the forbidden tree, they were punished by God. Their eternal sentence was to be subservient to men.

Yet the words spoken by God in Genesis 3:16 occurred after the fall of humanity, after the disobedience of Adam and Eve, after the entrance of sin into the cosmic story. The question that should be raised is whether it is God's will for women to be ruled over by men or whether God is simply foretelling what the consequences of sin will be for humanity, specifically women, in this verse. The next two verses might shed some light upon this question. In them, God turns to man and curses the ground, stating that from now on man would have to till the cursed soil, only to produce "thorns and thistles." The garden, and the effortless fruits it produced, will be gone. Only through the sweat of the brow will Adam be fed. Again, does this mean that it is the will of God for Adam and all of his descendants to work and labor in sorrow? No, of course not. It is God's will for Adam to continue living in the garden, being one with his wife and his Creator.

By the same token, we ask if it is God's will that women be ruled over by men. Again, using the same reasoning, the answer must be no. It is God's will to return women to the garden, where "they were both naked, yet they were not ashamed," where the relationship between the man and the woman was vulnerable yet safe, because no power relationship existed between them. Genesis 3:16 does not describe God's curse on women, any more than Genesis 3:17 does not describe God's curse on men. In both of these verses, God is foretelling the consequences of sin. Both the man and the woman wanted to be like God, so they ate the mango; both desired the power that came with being God. Instead, they have fallen to a state where social structures are created to deny them the power they sought: subservience to economic structures (agriculture as a way of surviving) for men, and sexist relational structures for women. It is not that God ordains, approves of, or condones these new structural relationships but, rather, that their development is part of the natural evolution of humanity's fall.

But doesn't Genesis 2:18 say that the woman was created for the man to be his helpmate? "And Yahweh God said, 'It is not good for the man to be alone; I will make for him a helper suited for him.'" The Hebrew word used in the text, *ezer*, usually translated as "helpmate," comes from the root word meaning "support" or "help." But the usage of *ezer* does not imply subordination or inferiority for the one who is doing the helping. For example, in Exodus 18:4, God is referred to as the "God of my fathers [who] was my *helper*." In Psalm 10:14, the psalmist proclaims God as being the "*helper* of the orphans," and in Psalm 118:7, the psalmist declares, "The Lord is with me, God is my *helper*." In none of these cases, nor in any of the other places throughout the Bible where God is referred to as our helper, does *ezer* imply subservience. Why then do we assume it when *ezer* is used to describe the woman? Several female biblical scholars insist that a better translation of *ezer*, as used in the Genesis passage, is the word "companion," which connotes woman as a counterpart to man.

What is God's desire for the relationship that should exist between men and women? For this, we turn to the first creation story, specifically Genesis 1:27:[1] "And God created the *adam* in God's image, in God's image God created it, male and female God created them." Most Bibles translate the Hebrew word *adam* as "man," hence rendering the verse as "God created man in God's image." Yet the word *adam* can have three different meanings. It can mean Adam, a proper name, in this case, Adam the husband of Eve. Or the word *adam* can be translated as "man," a male-gendered individual, as opposed to the word "woman." Finally, the word can also mean mankind, as in all of humanity.

If we translate *adam* to mean a man, as opposed to a woman, we must ask if this created man was both male and female? No, of course not.[2] What if we were to translate *adam* to mean humanity? Is humanity male and female? Yes, both males and females make up humanity. Thus, I suggest that God created humanity in God's own image, male and female God created them. The image of God is both male and female, for both sexes find their model in the Deity.

Both Jews and Christians have historically proclaimed that their God has no bodily form, hence no gender. The masculine pronoun attributed to God has less to do with "correct" theological thought and more to do with the patriarchal bias of biblical writers who attribute a "he" to God. Yet, to refer to God solely in the masculine limits and confines the mystery that is God to a human-made image. God is both male and female, and thus God is neither male nor female.

If God created male and female in God's own image, then both the man and the woman are equal within God's eyes because both are patterned after God. Women cease to be a copy of a man, an appendix to a story centered on the man's need for companionship. The fall of humanity, due to Adam and Eve's action, changed this mutually equal relationship. One of the consequences of sin was its manifestation in the form of sexism, where the woman ceased to be a person in the image of God and became instead a possession to be owned by the man. The transformation of women into objects for possession is reflected throughout the Hebrew Scriptures. The tenth commandment demonstrates how a woman, like a house, slave, ox, or donkey, is a possession of the male.

> You shall not covet your neighbor's house; you shall not covet your neighbor's wife, or his male slave, or his slave girl, or his ox, or his donkey, or anything which belongs to your neighbor. (Ex. 20:17)

Women as possessions were a means by which a man's honor within society could be lost. The taking of another man's woman brought shame to the household and family name of the man whose possession was taken. Consequently, adultery only applied to the married or betrothed woman who engaged in sexual relationships with anyone other than her husband. If a woman was caught in the act of adultery, she could face a death sentence. John 8:3–11 tells the story of a woman, "caught in the very act of committing adultery," who was brought to Jesus. It is interesting to note that the man with whom she was adulterous was not called to task. Why wasn't he also brought before Jesus? Because it was her sin, not his.

In the Hebrew Scriptures, a man was guilty only if he had sexual relationships with another man's wife, that is, another man's possession. With this one exception, a married man was free to engage in sexual relationships with nonmarried women. When King David was punished for his adulterous relationship with

Bathsheba, it was not because he engaged in a sexual relationship outside marriage. David's sin was against Uriah, Bathsheba's husband, because David took his possession, his wife Bathsheba. This is made clear in the prophet's condemnation of David in which he compares the king to the rich man with an abundant flock who steals the only lamb of a poor man. Bathsheba, like the lamb, was the object taken from the "true" victim, Uriah (2 Sam. 12:1–4).

As possessions, women could also be given as ransom for men. This happened more than once, as in the city of Sodom, where Abraham's nephew Lot lived. One night, when Lot had received unknown visitors, the men of Sodom surrounded his house and banged on the door, crying out, "Where are the men who came to you tonight? Send them out to us that we may abuse and rape them!" But Lot went out to them and said,

> My brothers, please do not act evilly. See now, I have two daughters who have never known a man. Please let me bring them out to you, and do to them as you see fit. Only do not do a thing to these men, because they have come under the shadow of my roof. (Gen. 19:7–8)

In Lot's mind, his daughters were worth far less than the two strangers, only because the strangers were men.

There is a similar scenario in Judges 19–21. On his journey home, a Levite, along with his concubine, stopped in the town of Gibeah, which belonged to the tribe of Benjamin. An old man of the town offered hospitality to the Levite and welcomed him to his house. When night fell, the men of the city came banging at his door, demanding that the Levite be sent out so that the townsmen could have their way with him. The old man went out to meet them and, like Lot, offered his virgin daughter and the Levite's concubine as a ransom, insisting that the men of the town do with them whatever they saw fit. They took the concubine, raped her, and left her lying at the door of the house where the Levite slept. The next morning the Levite arose to find his concubine lying on the floor. He placed her on his donkey and continued his journey home. When he arrived at his house, he took a knife and cut her into twelve pieces, sending her dismembered body parts to the borders of Israel. When the rest of Israel saw what occurred, they were outraged at the wickedness of the people of Gibeah, from the tribe of Benjamin, because they had violated the Levite's possession.

All of Israel then went to war against the tribe of Benjamin. After winning the battle, the rest of Israel swore never to give their daughters to the Benjamites as wives. Yet they regretted their oath, for it meant the loss of one of the twelve tribes. In the end, the other tribes of Israel, after great bloodshed, captured four hundred virgins from Jabesh-gilead who were then given as wives to the six hundred surviving Benjamites. The rape of one has now become the rape of four hundred. However, there were not enough virgins to go around, so they instructed the Benjamites to lie in wait in the vineyards of the town of Shiloh, and when their young maidens came to dance during the Lord's feast, the Benjamites were to catch a wife for themselves and take them back to their land. Hence the kidnaping and subsequent rape of these young maidens resolved the honor of the men who swore not to give their possessions (daughters) in marriage to the Benjamites.

This story is disturbing for several reasons. First, the Bible is silent about the identity of the concubine. She is remembered only as an unnamed object. As a possession, her name, identity, or story are unimportant. The narrative never reveals her voice or her humanity. Second, the giving of the virgin daughter and the "seasoned" concubine indicates the low station of women. Rape of men by men was considered a vile thing, but rape of women by men was more acceptable. Third, conflicts between men, whether between the old man and the Gibeah townsmen or between the tribes of Israel and the survivors of the tribe of Benjamin, could be resolved through the sacrifice of women. Fourth, rape of the woman was not the crime that defined the wickedness of the Benjamites; rather, their sin was the violation of the Levite's property. Fifth, the Hebrew text does not state whether the concubine was dead or alive after being raped all night. The silence of the text indicates that it really didn't matter if she was alive or dead, for, after all, her owner could dispose of his possession as he chose. Like Christ, her body was broken, and literally given for many. Sixth, the battle that ensued from the rape of one concluded in the offering of four hundred maidens to be raped by the surviving Benjamite soldiers and the taking of two hundred more maidens. Finally, the most disturbing aspect of the narrative is the silence of God. Nowhere does the text provide comfort to the abused women or to the reader of the story. Nowhere are we informed of how God viewed these atrocities. No reassuring words demonstrate God's contempt for such actions. The unnamed concubine is neither the first nor the last example that demonstrates how women were reduced to objects within the Hebrew Bible.[3] Women like Tamar, the daughter-in-law of Judah; Tamar, the daughter of King David; the unnamed daughter of Jephthah; or the virgins of the town of Midian who were taken as booty on Moses' order— all provide disturbing narratives of female marginality.

Because of patriarchy, a woman who belonged to one man yet was used by another brought shame to the honor of the man who owned her. Hence, to protect his honor, the man confined the woman to the household, where she was secure from dishonoring her husband. By the same token, if her husband's authority was to be challenged by a political or social rival, the best way to announce the challenge publically was to take control of his possessions, specifically his women. This concept is demonstrated in 2 Samuel 15–16. In these passages, David's authority as king was challenged by his son Absalom. Absalom mounted a rebellion that forced David to flee Jerusalem. Upon entering the city, Absalom, on the advice of his counselor Ahithopel, thought of a way in which Absalom could consolidate his power and authority. The solution: he pitched a tent on the palace's housetop, in the sight of all Israel, and raped all of his father's concubines. This was not a sexual act motivated by lust; rather, women were the means by which Absalom could wrestle authority from his father. Absalom literally provided public notice that he had taken his father's place and was now in control of his father's possessions.

A survey of the Law clearly shows how patriarchy is anchored in the Bible: 1) If a Hebrew man was sold into slavery, he served for six years, after which time he could leave with no compensation due. Female Hebrew slaves had to be bought back (Ex. 21:1–11). 2) A man who seduced (raped) a virgin had to either marry her or pay her father a fixed sum. Additionally, the victim of the seduction was not the virgin; rather it was her father, and so it was he who received compensation for the "spoiling" of his property (Ex. 22:15–16). 3) The firstborn son (or male animal) was consecrated unto the Lord; not so for the firstborn daughter

(Deut. 15:19–23). 4) Three times a year only the menfolk had to present themselves before God during the great national feasts. Women did not have to do so (Ex. 23:14–19). 5) Women could not serve as priests, and priests could only marry virgins (Lev. 21:1–9). 6) A woman's parents had to prove their daughter was a virgin when she climbed into her new husband's bed (Deut. 22:13–21). No such requirements of sexual purity were expected of men. 7) If a man made a vow to God, he had to keep it, but if a woman made a vow, her father or husband had veto powers that could void the vow (Num. 30:1–17). 8) Women were frequently excluded from participating in Temple rituals and festivals due to the "uncleanliness" of their menstruation cycle (Lev. 15:19). 9) Only if a man died without having any sons would his inheritance pass to his daughters (Num. 27:8–9). 10) Women could be taken as war booty (Deut. 21:10–14). 11) A woman who gave birth to a boy was "unclean" for fourteen days, but if she gave birth to a girl, she was unclean for twice as long (Lev. 12:1–5). 12) Men could have multiple sex partners, even to the point of maintaining a harem. Women could only have one sex partner (Lev. 18:18). 13) A husband who suspected his wife of infidelity could have her ingest a bitter elixir before the priest—if she survived, she was faithful; if she was afflicted, she was guilty of adultery (Num. 5:11–31). Men did not need to drink such brews.

Probably the most blatant abuse of sexism was the determination of the value of a person dedicated by a vow to God. According to Leviticus 27:1–8, the value of men between the ages of twenty and sixty years was fifty silver shekels, while a woman was only worth thirty. If the men were over sixty years of age, then their worth dropped to fifteen shekels, while the worth of women dropped to ten. One is left questioning if these laws were indeed the will of God or if these were the laws of men who attributed the regulations to God in order to protect their power and privilege within patriarchy. If these regulations came from God, then God stands accused of sexism.

It appears that the Bible advocates patriarchal structures. At the very least, it has been used to justify sexism. How can liberation be found in what feminist biblical scholar Phyllis Trible calls these texts of terror? We are told that King Solomon, the wisest man who ever lived, had three hundred wives and six hundred concubines. Can a biblical case be made for polygamy and concubinage? Of course not—we automatically assume that these particular social structures are not relevant for the modern era. Additionally, we consciously or subconsciously make a distinction between the Bible advocating a particular social structure and the Bible simply describing the social practices of its time. Yet, how do we justify in our own minds the rejection of social structures such as polygamy and concubinage while still advocating the overall foundation of patriarchy? Is patriarchy also a structure that the liberating Good News of Jesus demands that his disciples flatly reject? To answer this question, we turn to the New Testament.

Sexism from the Margins

One of the regulations of the Law not mentioned above deals with divorce. According to Deuteronomy 24:1–2, a husband could dismiss his wife simply by serving her with a written bill of divorce. The grounds for divorce could be minor, based on something she did that was considered improper or even on a general dislike of her. By the time of Jesus, the practice had developed whereby a husband was able to divorce his wife for whatever reason he chose, yet no Levitical law existed that allowed women to initiate divorce procedures. Divorce was a male privilege. Matthew 19:3–9, however, provides a model for interpreting patriarchal passages like Deuteronomy 24:1–2, as well as the other biblical verses that contribute to the marginalization of women. The Matthew passage reads as follows:

> And the Pharisees approached [Jesus], tempting him by saying, "Is it lawful for a man to dismiss his wife for whatever reason?" And he answered them, "Did you not read that God made them male and female from the beginning? And God said, 'For this reason a man shall leave his father and mother, and be joined to his wife, and the two shall be one flesh.' So they are no longer two, but one flesh. What God has yoked together, let no one separate." They said to him, "Why then did Moses command to give a bill of divorce, and put her away?" He said to them, "In view of your hardheartedness, Moses allowed you to put away your wives, but from

the beginning it was not so. And I say to you, that whosoever puts away his wife, with the exception of fornication, and marries another commits adultery. And the one who marries a divorcée commits adultery."

In the above passage, Jesus dismisses the Deuteronomic law because of the social context in which it was written, a context in which the "hardheartedness" of men who benefited from sexism took preference over the intended will of the Creator expressed in the first two chapters of Genesis. Laws like Deuteronomy 24:1–2 are, according to Jesus, the product of men establishing sinful patriarchal hierarchies, rather than God's perfect will that men and women coexist as companions.

Can Christians follow Jesus' example and dismiss biblical verses, like the ones previously mentioned, if they cause oppression? In chapter 2, we concluded by stating that the entire Bible should be read through the lens of the gospel message, specifically through passages like John 10:10, where Jesus states, "I came that they may have life, and have it abundantly." If verses within the Bible advocate the subjugation of one person to another and hence prevent life from being lived abundantly by a segment of the population, then those verses are anti-gospel and must be reinterpreted in light of the fullest revelation of God found in Christ. Insistence on reading the text solely through the eyes of men violates the gospel message of liberation, as women are forced to conform to patriarchal traditions that rob them of their dignity. Women who read the text with their own eyes are simply no longer willing to accept biblical interpretations constructed by men as normative for their lives. In short, as demonstrated in Matthew 19:3–9, Jesus becomes the model by which Christians read, interpret, and accept (or dismiss) verses that appear to justify oppressive social structures.

Feminism among Women of Color

Women of color face multiple oppressors. They must learn how to survive in a society that privileges Euroamericans as well as privileges men. Like their Euroamerican sisters, they struggle for genuine respect of their personhood. As a result, they emphasize their social location while valuing their experiences as a source and lens for reading the biblical text. Yet, unlike their Euroamerican sisters, they must also face racial and ethnic discrimination from the dominant culture along with sexism from within their own marginalized group, where all too often Euroamerican men and men of color agree on the so-called biblical mandate that subordinates women. In addition, their Euroamerican sisters, who also confront sexism, may very easily become their oppressors as they achieve some equal opportunities with men in certain roles, roles that privilege the dominant culture at the expense of those existing on the margins of society.

Women of color often question some feminist approaches toward liberation, fearing that the term is being used to mean equality with white middle- and upper-class males. Such equality means equal opportunities in employment and education and being viewed as equals before the law. Although inequality in opportunities is unacceptable, oppression (or discrimination) and liberation can never be limited to Euroamerican definitions. Then liberation is reduced to political maneuvering within society where marginalized groups attempt to create new power bases and often struggle against each other. Such movements ignore the disproportionate distribution of wealth and overall racism in society. This is why women of color challenge Euroamerican feminists to resist becoming another group competing for its respective rights within a balance of power based on conflicting interests, interests that at times collide with those of people of color (both female and male).

The failure of some Eurocentric feminist groups to distinguish between liberation and the quest for equality with Euroamerican middle- and upper-class men has kept some feminist movements from truly fostering liberation. The type of liberation that many women of color seek encompasses freedom from oppressive economic, political, and social conditions for themselves and their communities (including their fathers, husbands, and sons). Women of color seek within the Scriptures stories that empower them to take control of their lives, bodies, and destiny, stories that show that their struggle is sometimes with women of the dominant culture. This approach to the Bible calls for women of color to collaborate with all oppressed groups to fundamentally change the economic, political, and social structures of society and to cultivate a spiritual dimension of liberation through a reading of the

Scriptures that challenges traditional biblical interpretations. Women of color reading the Bible from the margins can confront the prevalent sexism within their own ethnic and racial community as well as the racial, ethnic, and class prejudice within the Euroamerican feminist community.

Crucial to women of color is the story of Hagar, the Egyptian slave girl of Sarah (Abraham's wife), recorded in Genesis 16:1–16 and 21:9–21. Hagar was marginalized by gender, ethnicity, and class. While most white women identify with Sarah, the matriarch in the story and the mother of the faith, most women of color resonate with the experiences of Hagar. Abraham and Sarah, who were wealthy, attributed their riches to God's blessings. Still, Sarah, like other women of her time, was considered property that could be sacrificed as needed. Remember, at least twice Abraham tried to pass her off as his sister in order to protect himself, meaning that she could have been accosted by the men of the towns through which they passed (Gen. 13:12–19; 20). Unfortunately, if the original structures of oppression are not dismantled, those who are oppressed can easily become oppressors. Sarah, the property of her husband, obtained her own property in the form of Hagar, a resident alien.

Sarah's inability to bear Abraham children led her to conclude that her barrenness was a curse by God, and so she took matters into her own hands. In keeping with the customs of her time, she offered her servant, a slave girl, as an instrument by which Abraham could sire an heir. Hagar, as womb, not person, was used to accomplish the goals of those who owned her body. Her body and labor existed to be exploited by those who had power over her. If a woman does not have control over her sexual organs and is forced to have sexual relationships with a man against her will, for whatever reason, the result is called rape. Hagar, as a slave, as property, was required to "perform" at the will of her owners, a familiar scenario for many black female slaves who, as possessions, had to satisfy their master's desires as well as face the dehumanizing practice of being "rented out" to other white men as concubines.

As the story proceeds, the unexpected happened. Sarah's property, a surrogate mother, experienced consciousness raising and recognized her own dignity. Hagar became the first woman in the Bible to seek her own liberation, by fleeing Sarah's cruelty (as well as sexual rivalry between barrenness and fertility). She thus chose death in the desert, if necessary, to challenge the power structures that oppressed her, even though she was pregnant by Abraham. While in the wilderness, Hagar was visited by a messenger of God, a God who accompanied the outcast in the midst of her unwarranted suffering. Yet the divine message for Hagar was to return to Sarah and "suffer affliction under her hand." Why would God require her to return to slavery? Perhaps it was crucial for the survival of her unborn son, who would then be born in the house of Abraham an heir to the promise of God. But is this liberation or a strategy for survival? Regardless, her child becomes an intruder to the covenant. It is to be noted that, breaking with biblical tradition, God's promise was made to a woman, with no reference to a man.

At this point, Hagar, the lowly marginalized woman, does the unexpected: she dares to give God a name, a privilege extended to no other person throughout the Bible. Ancient custom dictated that only a superior could name those who are lower in status, yet here a slave woman is the first biblically recorded person to give God a name. She calls God *El Roi,* the God who sees, uniting the divine with her human experience of suffering.

The second time the Bible returns to Hagar, she has been cast out by those who own her. Sarah's jealousy got the better of her. Fearful that her son's inheritance could be jeopardized by Abraham's firstborn, Ishmael, she connived to have him and his mother, Hagar, forced into exile. Again Hagar found herself in the desert facing death, thrown out as an old used object no longer needed by its owner, a familiar scenario for most domestic servants today. Homeless because of the unwillingness of the father of her child to shoulder his responsibility, she was abandoned, like so many women of color today. Alone in the desert, facing death, and questioning the promise God previously uttered about the multitude of her descendants, she must have wondered about the blindness of the God who sees. Yet, this time, God heard the cry of her son and rescued them.

Hagar suffered from classism (a slave), racism (an Egyptian foreigner), and sexism (a woman raped by Abraham). Because of her status, Hagar becomes a lens by which the biblical text can be read, a reading that focuses on the struggle for liberation and survival with dignity. This story of the used and abused woman is a motif that resonates with many women of color. Even natural allies, women of the dominant culture like Sarah, capitalize on her body. Nevertheless, God is found in the midst of the struggle of those relegated to the margins, even when these religious patriarchs of the faith have participated in their marginalization! Because God chooses to accompany those who are disenfranchised, Hagar and her child Ishmael complicated the history of salvation by becoming part of God's promise to make a nation by using Abraham's seed. Women of color continue to "complicate" how the dominant culture interprets God's promises.[4]

JUSTIFYING HOMOPHOBIA

The sin of Sodom is an abomination before God. It is a prevalent sin within our society and undermines Christianity. Its constant practice contributes to the downfall of civilization and leads nations toward barbarism. It is the responsibility of all who call themselves Christian to root out this sin from society and dedicate themselves to abolishing this defiled practice. Because the elimination of this sin is crucial for participating in the abundant life, it is important that we correctly define what the sin of Sodom is. Regardless of how the dominant culture interprets the Genesis story of God's wrath falling upon Sodom and Gomorrah, the Bible's definition of the sin of Sodom is vastly different from what is usually preached from most pulpits throughout the land.

According to Genesis 19, two angels sent to Sodom found hospitality in the house of Lot (Abraham's nephew). Later in the evening, the men of the town went to Lot's house, demanding that the two strangers be handed over to them so that they could *know* them ("to know" being a euphemism for having a sexual relationship). Lot refused, but he offered his two virgin daughters, as discussed above. When the men attempted to take the two strangers by force, the angels struck them with blindness. They then warned Lot and his family to flee the city because it would be destroyed by God. Lot and his family escaped while fire and brimstone rained down on Sodom and Gomorrah. These cities of iniquity were destroyed for their wickedness, interpreted by many as the practice of homosexuality on the basis that the men of Sodom wanted to rape the two strangers.

Several gay or lesbian Christians claim that Genesis 19 does not condemn homosexuality. While they acknowledge that in several places throughout the Scriptures Sodom is used as a symbol signifying evil, they insist that in none of these instances does the Bible specifically refer to homosexuality or link it to Sodom. What then was the sin of Sodom? According to the prophet Ezekiel:

> Behold, this was the iniquity of your sister Sodom: pride, fullness of bread, and abundance of idleness were in her and her daughters. She did not strengthen the hand of the poor or the needy. Also, they were haughty and did abomination before me. (16:49)

For Ezekiel, Sodom's sin was its unwillingness, due to its pride and haughtiness, to share its abundance with those who were poor and marginalized. This haughtiness becomes the root cause of the abomination it does before God. For the prophet Isaiah, the acts that Israel was then committing were the same acts that led to the destruction of Sodom and Gomorrah. Referring to Israel as Sodom and Gomorrah, the prophet Isaiah says,

> Hear the word of Yahweh, O rulers of Sodom, listen to the law of our God, O people of Gomorrah! What use is it to me your many sacrifices? . . . Your palms are full of blood. Wash yourselves, purify yourselves, remove the evil of your doings before my eyes. Cease doing evil. Learn to do good. Seek justice, reprove the oppressor, judge the orphan, contend for the widow. (1:10–17)

Again the crime of Sodom and Gomorrah is described as a lack of justice done in the name of the orphans and widows. In a patriarchal society, the most vulnerable members are those who are not under the care of a man, specifically the orphan who has lost her or his father and the widow who has lost her husband. Deprived of a male protector, they cease to hold any standing in a male-centered society; this is why the Bible makes their care the responsibility of all the people. Caring for the orphan and widow refers to the most marginalized members of the community. The downfall of Sodom, according to Isaiah, was its refusal to bring justice to the disenfranchised.

Sodom's sin, according to several gay and lesbian scholars, was the lack of hospitality shown by the dominant culture to those who resided in the margins. In the biblical world, hospitality meant more than simply being neighborly. Hospitality went beyond the entertainment of friends and family; rather, it was a carefully orchestrated social practice to receive strangers and make them guests. Because strangers lacked legal standing when visiting a community, their survival at times depended on falling under the protection of an established community member who would serve as host. Sodom's offense was its refusal to recognize these ancient social traditions, which brought dishonor upon not only Lot's guests but also Lot's household. The prophets reminded the people of these ancient traditions and warned the people that hospitality was to be extended to the marginalized. Dishonoring the orphan, the widow, the alien, in short those who were marginalized, became the mark of a godless nation.

Any interpretation of the Genesis 19 passage is further complicated when it is recognized that no specific equivalent exists in the Hebrew (or Greek) text for the word "homosexual." In fact, no biblical word exists whose meaning remotely defines the essence of how the contemporary word "homosexuality" is used. Both the Hebrew and the Greek texts use idioms causing any interpretation of the passage to be fraught with difficulties. The term "homosexual" did not even come into existence until the nineteenth century. The word "sodomy" did not enter the English language until the thirteenth century, and even then was not always connected with anal intercourse, as it is today. In different historical periods, sodomy has meant everything from anal copulation among men, to acts of heterosexual oral sex, to bestiality.

Defining homosexuality is further complicated when we recognize that different modern cultures understand the word "homosexual" in different ways. For example, among Euroamericans, two men who engage in a same-sex act are both called homosexuals. Yet, in other world cultures, only the one who places himself in the "position" of a woman is deemed to be gay. In fact, the man who is in the dominant position during the sex act is at times able to retain, if not increase, his manliness. The phenomenon of labeling only one of the men in a sexual act "gay" is detected within the U.S. prison system, where rape enhances the power and manliness of the penetrator while the one who is dominated is deprived of manly honor and dignity. This may be the way homosexuality was understood during biblical times. The Greek word for homosexuality used in the New Testament literally means "soft," raising questions as to who is the homosexual: both male partners or just the one who places himself in a "soft" position? When we search the Scriptures in order to learn about teachings on homosexuality, we need to recognize that the term has historically signified different concepts.

These uncertainties concerning the words for, and concepts of, homosexuality suggest a danger in juxtaposing ancient biblical prohibitions with contemporary sexual milieus without considering the historical and cultural social location from which these prohibitions arose. Nonetheless, one of the most contentious issues facing the churches today deals with homosexuality. Yet there are only a few instances where the Bible refers to same-sex intercourse: Leviticus 18:22 and 20:13 and Deuteronomy 23:17–18 in the Hebrew Bible; Romans 1:26–27, 1 Corinthians 6:9, and Timothy 1:10 in the New Testament. The question we will now explore is how gays and lesbians understand and interpret these biblical texts.

An initial glance reveals a lack of textual references to same-sex intercourse throughout the Hebrew Bible. In fact, no reference to lesbianism exists in the Hebrew Bible, only same-sex male relationships. These two Leviticus passages (18:22 and 20:13) are embedded in what scholars call the Holiness Code, which encompasses Leviticus 17 through 26. In these chapters, the Israelites are warned not to copy practices of the Canaanites that would make them unclean, as in the case of the preparation and eating of food, rituals of worship, cleanliness, and so forth. Such actions, including having sexual intercourse with a menstruating woman or *mishkav zachur,* literally, "lying with a male," are considered *to'eivah,* an abomination, a technical cultic term for uncleanliness. The Holiness Code's main objective was to serve as a warning for the Israelites against following the practices of the inhabitants of the land they would possess. For some gay and lesbian biblical scholars, these forms of sexual prohibitions are no more significant to the contemporary Christian than the dietary regulations concerning pork or shellfish. The Gospels become the means by which Christians interpreted and still interpret the Hebrew Bible, rendering certain passages nonbinding, as in the case of the dietary laws. Christians also ignore other passages of the Hebrew Bible that call for non-Christian acts, as in the case of Deuteronomy 7:1–5, which calls for genocide.

Although Deuteronomy 23:17–18 appears to be a recast of the earlier passage in Leviticus, some gay Christians insist that its focus was instead on the cult prostitution, which included homosexual activities as part of the rituals. The prohibition is against both heterosexual and homosexual activities that have been ritualized for the purpose of worshiping foreign gods. These verses contribute little if any information about the Jewish view of homosexuality because the text is dealing with cult prostitution, not same-sex mutual relationships. Modern-day homosexuality is not connected to idolatry.[5]

Turning our attention to the book of Romans, we notice that it does not begin with a discourse against homosexuality but rather with a thesis against pagan religions that replace created things for the Creator. Paul writes in the first chapter, "[For they] exchanged the glory of the incorruptible God for a likeness of an image of corruptible man, and birds, and four-footed animals, and reptiles" (v. 23). These verses, like those of Deuteronomy, are references to cult practices typical of pagan religions that promoted homosexual and heterosexual promiscuity.[6]

At first glance it appears that homosexuality is also mentioned in 1 Corinthians 6:9 and 1 Timothy 1:10. Yet the homosexual model prevalent during Paul's time was one in which preadolescent boys were exploited by adult males for the purpose of the adult's sexual gratification. Could these two passages be referring not to same-sex relationships between two adult males but to a form of pederasty, generally disapproved of in Greco-Roman and Jewish literature?[7]

Homophobia from the Margins

Many gay and lesbian Christians question if companionship is limited only to heterosexual relationships. At the very least, we must consider that claims of biblical condemnation of same-sex mutual affection and love are questionable. Many Christians are not totally convinced that biblical verses that mention homosexuality are referring to its modern practice. In fact, gay and lesbian Christians have begun reading the Scriptures to reconcile the sexual orientation of their birth with their faith in Christ Jesus.

For example, at first glance it appears that Jesus makes no reference to homosexuality. But several gay biblical scholars have pointed to Matthew 19:12: "For there are eunuchs who are born thus from their mother's womb, and there are eunuchs who are made eunuchs by men, and there are eunuchs who make themselves eunuchs for the sake of the reign of heaven." Those who are made eunuchs, like Nehemiah the cupbearer, are those who were castrated in order to work for the king. This process insured their ability to serve in the royal household without jeopardizing the "honor" of the king through dishonoring his possessions, specifically his queen or harem. Those who chose to be eunuchs for the sake of God's reign are those who chose celibacy as a religious calling. But how do we interpret what it means to be a eunuch from birth? Some gay scholars believe that this verse refers to them as modern-day sexual outcasts or to transgendered persons. According to these scholars, the eunuchs from birth may represent men who have not had sexual relationships with women because of their orientation from birth.

Eunuchs were considered spiritual outcasts, unable to participate in the cultic practices of the faith community: "He shall not enter the assembly of Yahweh if his male member is wounded, crushed, or cut" (Deut. 23:1).[8] By referring to himself as a eunuch, it could be said that Jesus seeks solidarity with the sexually oppressed of his times while fulfilling the promise stated in Isaiah:

Do not let the eunuch say, "Behold, I am a dried up tree," for thus says Yahweh to the eunuchs who keep my Sabbaths, and choose things with which I am pleased, and take hold of my covenant. I will even give them in my house and in my walls a hand and a name better than sons and daughters; I will give them an everlasting name which shall not be cut off. (56:3–5)

Jesus' inclusion of the sexual outcast served as a model for welcoming and affirming everyone into the early Christian church. Love for all people, including the outcasts, becomes the acceptable norm established by Jesus. Love is an action word, not an abstract concept based on unexpressed feelings. The real tests of love are that it be unconditional, and that it be love for the sake of the person, as she or he is. When the disciple Philip (according to Acts 8:26–40) encounters an Ethiopian eunuch on the road to Gaza who is reading the prophet Isaiah, Philip is quick to share the affirming message of the gospel and to welcome the sexual outcast, in spite of the Law (Deut. 23:1), into the fellowship of believers.

THE HERMENEUTICAL CIRCLE

In chapter 2 we explored how the Bible is read from the center of power and privilege. The present chapter, along with chapter 3, has explored how marginalized groups, in their search for liberation and justice, interpret Scripture. How exactly do the center and the margins differ in reading and interpreting biblical texts? For most faith communities within the dominant culture, the Bible is viewed and understood as containing or being universal truth, accessible to Protestants and to Catholics alike. In both traditions, the Bible is the expression of the will of God that determines what is to be believed (theology) and how its readers are to conduct their lives (praxis). Biblical interpretation is deductive; that is, the universal truth of the Bible or the teachings of the church is the starting point, a first step that leads to a second step, which is the application of biblical truth. Yet what happens when biblical truth is fused and confused with interpretations made by a dominant culture? Are interpretations from the center of society, often concerned with the preservation and maintenance of the status quo, which provides privilege, indeed biblical truth? If the center's interpretations are but constructed opinions rather than definitive statements, then applications deducted from those opinions can be harmful and oppressive to those who do not reside in the center.

Most people who read the Bible from the margins reverse this methodology. Oppressed groups begin with their need for liberation. Engagement in a praxis (action) of liberation informs them how biblical texts are to be interpreted. This interpretation then informs and strengthens any new praxis. This new praxis leads the Christian to a clearer understanding of the Bible that informs any further praxis. Biblical interpretation, then, becomes a reflection of liberative action. While such an approach may be perceived with disdain by those accustomed to interpreting the text from within the scholarly community, reading the Bible from the margins has contributed to the development of a theological perspective that emphasizes the social and living context of those who are doing the reading. The everyday experiences manifested in art, community relationships, popular religious expressions, and cultural customs become the lens through which the Bible is understood.

Using this methodology, biblical interpretations are no longer stagnant. They are continuously forced to change as the present-day realities faced by both the individual and society change; it is those realities that dictate how the Bible is to be read in order to guide those who struggle. Each new and changing reality forces the Christian to interpret God's word afresh and return to the text again to reinterpret God's word.[9] For those who are disenfranchised, in this way the reality of life's hardships and oppression continually intersects with the biblical message of hope and liberation. Interpreting the Bible is forever linked with a commitment to critically analyze society so as to bring it closer to the justice of the reign of God. Learning to read the Bible from the margins allows individuals like Ruvimbo, the young African who was forced to change his name to John when he became a Christian, to interpret the Bible so that it can be relevant to his life as an African.

As for Ruvimbo, when I last saw him, he was going through the process of changing his legal documents back to Ruvimbo. If one of the first acts of liberation is to name oneself apart from the name given by those in power, then Ruvimbo has begun to take this step. Once he sees himself through his own eyes, he will also be better equipped to see Jesus. Any reading of the Bible from the margins of society requires an understanding of who Jesus is. Jesus, as God's fullest revelation of God to humanity, guides readers of the biblical text in understanding the divine character in the daily injustices of everyday life. The next chapter will explore how Jesus is seen and understood from the margins, a way of seeing that is as crucial for the dominant culture's salvation as it is for the groups that exist on the margins.

CHAPTER 5

Who Do You Say I Am?

During Holy Week of 2001, the Discovery Channel and the British Broadcasting Corporation coproduced a television documentary titled *Jesus: The Complete Story*. While some interpretations based on so-called recent scientific discoveries were questionable, of interest was the attempt to re-create Jesus' physical appearance. Using a two-thousand-year-old Jewish skull, a forensic artist created a computer-generated image of what Jesus might have looked like. Skin pigmentation and hair color were based on third-century frescoes of Jewish faces found in ruins at Dura-Europos in Syria. The final image revealed an olive-skinned man with short dark curly hair. This image of Jesus challenged the traditional one that dates from the fifth century, as well as the more modern white-skinned, blue-eyed, blond-haired Jesus popularized on stained-glass windows and portraits.

For purposes of our inquiry, it really is unimportant if this reconstructed image represents how Jesus might have looked. Of greater interest is the reaction of some members of the dominant culture to this non-Eurocentric-looking Jesus, a reaction best illustrated by newspaper columnist Kathleen Parker of the Tribune Media Services in an article titled "Jesus Falls Victim to Makeover Madness." She bemoaned the fact that "this new Jesus looks like no one familiar. The willowy, long-haired figure who in picture books attracted children . . . now looks like the kind of guy who wouldn't make it through airport security." She was specifically disgusted with the new Jesus' jaw, which "looks likely to chomp down on a brontosaurus thigh," and his wide nose, which she calls "a snout that snorts." She longs for the Jesus of her "childhood Bible storybook." In short, she voices her anger that the white Jesus she grew up with is being replaced by an ethnic-looking Jesus, a Jesus who looks more like someone from the margins of society. She concludes by blasting the tendency of academic researchers to "debunk" the Aryan Jesus, insisting "that biblical revisionists won't be satisfied until they discover that Jesus was *really* a bisexual, cross-dressing, whale-saving, tobacco-hating, vegetarian African Queen who actually went to temple to lobby for women's rights."[1]

It is understandable that some from the dominant culture, like columnist Kathleen Parker, wish to maintain an image of a Jesus who, like them, is white. Yet, for the vast majority of people on the margins, a Jesus who is white does not necessarily represent salvation. For example, James Cone states that white theology cannot be Christian theology. Rather, it becomes a theology of white oppressors that provides divine sanction for criminal acts committed upon those who are oppressed.[2] As long as people on the margins bow their knees to a Christ who resembles their oppressors, people on the margins will also find themselves bowing before their oppressors. For Christ to have any power to liberate those who are disenfranchised, Jesus must be seen, perceived, and understood through the eyes of the marginalized. Such an action demands that the white Christ of the dominant culture, the Jesus of Kathleen Parker's childhood storybook Bible, be rejected by people from the margins, even though it may be an accepted image for Euroamericans.

In the early 1500s, Europeans in search of God, glory, and gold participated in the systematic process of eliminating Amerindians from the land they held communally. Upon arriving in what would eventually be called the Caribbean, these Christian men raped Amerindian women, disemboweled Amerindian children, and butchered Amerindian men. A local chieftain named Hatuey chose to resist the onslaught by creating a loose confederation of Amerindians to fight the invading colonizers. For three months he carried out a kind of guerrilla warfare, but he was eventually captured and condemned to death. As Hatuey was about to be burned at the stake, a Franciscan friar attempted to convert him to Christ with the promise of heaven and the threat of hell. Hatuey is reported to have asked if Christians went to heaven. The friar answered in the affirmative, and Hatuey retorted that he did not want to go to heaven, where he would see such cruel people.

Hatuey, along with many Amerindians, rejected the white Jesus of the dominant culture.

In 1619, a year before the *Mayflower* landed on Plymouth Rock and a few days after the first session of the Virginia House of Burgesses, the first slave ship docked in Virginia. It was named the *Jesus*. Prior to being led away from their homeland forever, Africans were forced to pass under a religious cleric who usually sat on an ivory chair baptizing these chained "heathens" in the name of Jesus. Throughout the Middle Passage, these slaves would see pious captains holding prayer services twice a day and penning famous hymns about the sweet name of Jesus or God's amazing grace. These Africans, being led to a life of servitude, like so many of their descendants, saw no reason to turn to the white Jesus of the dominant culture.

Like Amerindians and Africans, the people of the world have been told that there is only one true representation of Jesus and shown illustrations or images drawn by members of the dominant culture, such as columnist Kathleen Parker. This Jesus becomes a collective representation of society, a symbolic expression that provides a sense of unity and functions to solidify society. The Jesus of the dominant culture serves as a means by which those who are privileged transmit their culture, morality, and values from one generation to the next. It provides a divine symbolic mandate for models of social behavior designed to bless those with power who benefit from the status quo. Is it any wonder that the Kathleen Parkers of society find a nonwhite Jesus threatening?

The salvific gospel message of liberation incarnated in the life, death, and resurrection of Jesus Christ should be the criterion by which the Bible is to be interpreted. Unfortunately, through the white Jesus of the dominant culture, the opposite has occurred. The name of Jesus has been used historically to justify oppression and injustice. Here, then, is the basic question that people on the margins must ask when searching for the Christ who will serve as the touchstone for all biblical interpretations: does this image of Jesus Christ provide life and provide it abundantly? Rather than being a Jesus that provides abundant life, the white Jesus has been used to bring abundant death to those on the margins of society, and for this reason the white Jesus is rejected by some people on the margins because it has historically served as the Antichrist of

Christianity. The white Christ promised to the Amerindian about to be suffocated and the white Jesus whose name was blazoned upon the slave ship can symbolize for the people on the margins Satan, hiding in the image of an angel of light.

If the image of a white Christ symbolizes the religious sanction of oppressive societal structures, how should people on the margins perceive Jesus? Inevitably, every semester one of my students will ask me how I would physically describe Jesus. They really want me to comment on the color of his skin. Is it white? Black? Olive tone? I always respond in the same fashion: when I attempt to picture the incarnation, I envision Jesus as an old black Latina woman with AIDS. Why? The most disdained by society is the form the Deity takes. Because of racism, sexism, agism, and society's fear of AIDS, such a person is normatively avoided, ignored, and shunned. Yet in Matthew Jesus says that he is just that person: "Truly I say to you, inasmuch as you did it to one of these, the least of my people, you did it to me" (25:40). Jesus can be found among those whom society marginalizes. That homeless person you passed by this morning, avoiding eye contact, he is Jesus. The woman from the margins you refused to hire, the man of color cited by the police for driving under the influence of being nonwhite, the family from the margins who is charged higher interest and insurance rates— these are all Jesus. The person with AIDS whom we condemn, equating his or her infirmity with God's punishment, this person is also Jesus. All those people who make us uncomfortable because they do not belong to our race, ethnic group, or economic class embody Jesus. Jesus is reincarnated in the lives of those who are crucified today, a sacrifice so that those in power can continue to enjoy their privilege.

Jesus ties his being with those who are hungry, thirsty, naked, alien, imprisoned, and ill. Whatever Jesus may look like, he can be found in the struggle of the disenfranchised, not because they are holier but because they must struggle for the abundant life. If we want to describe Jesus' appearance, we need to describe the appearance of those who reside in the margins of society. If we want to commune with Christ, if we want to look into the eyes of the one we call Lord, then we can access him when we walk in solidarity, when we accompany the outcasts of society. For whatever is done or not done to one of these is done or not done to Jesus. This may be why the writer of Hebrews reminds us to show hospitality toward strangers, for "through this some may have unknowingly entertained angels" (13:2).

Because all people depict ultimate reality in a form native to their own culture, a Eurocentric Christ, although appropriate for the dominant culture, can seem powerless for people residing on the underside of that society. Because a Eurocentric Christ is incongruent with the reality that the disenfranchised are forced to occupy, salvation for them will be achieved when the white Christ of the dominant culture is rejected. To read, see, and define Christ from the margins is to make the message of the gospel relevant to those who are disenfranchised and trying to survive just one more day. As during the days of his earthly ministry, Jesus is not to be found among the religious elite who occupy the center of society, comfortable in their ornate cathedrals; rather he is found among the publicans, tax collectors, prostitutes, and sinners, in short, those who are considered outcasts by society. It is to the margins of society that we must go in order to find Jesus. The margins of society, in the here and now, in this time and place, are understood as encompassing the poor, Hispanics, Amerindians, Asian Americans, blacks, members of other disenfranchised groups, women, and gays.

THE ECONOMICALLY MARGINALIZED CHRIST

Who is this Jesus who was called Lord and Savior by those who suffered economically at the margins of society? Who is the Christ of the poor? The biblical text tells us that, although divine, he became human, assuming the condition of a slave, according to Paul's letter to the Philippians:

> [Jesus Christ], who subsisting in the form of God thought it not robbery to be equal with God, but emptied himself, taking the form of a slave, in the likeness of humans, and being found in the fashion of a human, he humbled himself, becoming obedient until death, even the death of the cross. (2:6–8)

The radicalness of the incarnation is not so much that the Creator of the universe became a frail human but rather that God chose

to become poor, to take the form of a slave. Jesus willingly assumed
the role of the ultradisenfranchised. He was born into, lived, and
died in poverty. Under our Christmas trees, among the multitude
of conspicuous gifts, we usually have a nativity scene. The baby
Jesus rests comfortably in a crib made of wood while angelic cows
gaze upon the miracle. The proud parents (Mary and Joseph) survey the sanitary scene as kings and peasants come to worship. Yet,
if we accept the reliability of the Gospels (particularly Matthew
and Luke), then Jesus was born in a barn, full of the manure of
those "angelic cows" and the flies attracted to most stables. A
manger was either a wooden box or a hole on the cave wall from
where horses and cattle ate. Like a barn animal, Mary was forced
to give birth amidst such unsanitary conditions. Jesus physically
entered this world as if he were homeless. This fact is not lost on
the poor of the earth, who recognize God's solidarity with them,
as articulated in the songs slaves sung:

> Poor little Jesus boy
> Made him to be born in a manger
> World treated him so mean
> Treats me mean too.[3]

To understand Jesus from the social location of the poor is to
create a sacred space where the marginalized can grapple with their
spiritual need to reconcile their God with their struggle for justice
and dignity. For many who read the Bible from the margins, Jesus'
poverty is attested by the sacrifice offered by his parents at his birth.
According to Luke, "And when the days of [Mary] cleansing were
fulfilled according to the Law of Moses . . . [they] offered a sacrifice according to the Law of the Lord, a pair of turtledoves, or two
young pigeons" (2:22–24). The law as stated in the twelfth chapter of the book of Leviticus required her to offer a lamb for her
child, but if she could not afford one, then the sacrifice would be
two turtledoves or two young pigeons. Mary made use of the offering of the poor.

Jesus' poverty was not limited to his birth. Jesus lived the life
of an itinerant preacher, a life marked by privation. Referring to
himself in Luke, Jesus would say, "The foxes have holes, and the
birds of the heaven nests, but the Son of man has nowhere to lay

his head" (9:58). He wandered throughout Judea without money in his purse. Several incidents indicating Jesus' lack of funds are recorded in the biblical text. For example, when questioned if he paid the didrachma (Temple tax), Jesus instructed Peter to find the necessary funds to pay the tax in the mouth of the first fish Peter hooked (Matt. 17:22–27). When asked if one should pay tribute to Caesar, Jesus asked to be shown a tribute coin rather than producing one himself (Luke 20:20–26). In order to survive financially, Jesus relied on the charity of others. "He traveled through every city and village . . . and the twelve were with him, also certain women . . . who were ministering to him of their possessions" (Luke 8:1–3).

Jesus also stressed his solidarity with the ultradisenfranchised by referring to himself as the good shepherd, as recorded in John 10:11. Today, when we think of a shepherd, we envision a wise, humble pastor who lovingly cares for his flock. Unfortunately, that was not how people saw shepherds during Jesus' time. No social status was so limited and tenuous, so close to no status at all, as that of the shepherd. The shepherd lived apart from what was considered civilization, among the company of the most miserable outcasts of society. From the margins, the shepherd occupied a slavelike space, usually guarding someone else's flock with his or her life.[4]

Then, too, Jesus came from the uncelebrated region of Galilee. Nazareth was so insignificant to the religious life of Judaism that the Hebrew Bible never mentions it. If it was not for Jesus being a Nazarene, Galilee may have been just another unknown and unimportant region of the world. To come from Galilee was considered by most in Jerusalem as being uncouth. The people of Jesus' time had such a low opinion of this provincial region that, according to John, when the multitudes discovered Jesus' origins, they exclaimed before abandoning him, "Are you not also from Galilee? Search the Scriptures and see that no prophet out of Galilee has been raised" (7:52–53). John also gives us the example of Nathaniel, one of Jesus' future disciples, who, upon learning Jesus was from Nazareth, showed his contempt by saying, "Can any good thing come out of Nazareth?" (1:46).

Can any good thing come out of the ghetto? Can any good thing come out of the *barrio*? Jesus came from the impure and mixed neighborhood of his time. No decent, respectable member of the center of society comes from *those* types of neighborhoods. Indeed, Jesus knows what it means to come from the "wrong side of the tracks"! Because he experienced the cultural bias of being from the margins of society, oppressed and poor people, including those of color, are able to find solidarity with their God.

To understand the message of Jesus, we are forced to look toward the margins of this society, to identify the heirs of Jesus' ministry. The writer of the epistle of James reminds us that God chose those who were poor: "Hear my beloved, did not God choose the poor of this world to be rich in faith and heirs to the reign which God promised to those loving God?"(2:5). It is to them that the reign of God is promised. It is they who can lead the center toward salvation, a concept that will be explored in greater detail in chapter 6. For now, it will suffice to stress that Christian churches that refuse to interpret biblical texts from the perspective of those who first heard the Gospels, the poor, end up fabricating interpretations that tend to spiritualize the gospel message and then refuse to deal literally with how those original hearers understood Christ.

For example, in Luke 12:16–21 Jesus tells the parable about a rich man who, having had a good harvest, decided to tear down his barns and build bigger ones to store his grain, thinking he could rest secure in his fortunes. Yet Jesus called him a fool because that very night he died and his riches did not save him; instead, they were left for others to enjoy. It appears as if Jesus is condemning people who attempt to forecast their potential gain, and position themselves so as to maximize on their investment by increasing storage space, even though they would be considered shrewd entrepreneurs by most of today's capitalist society. Today, we might want such an individual to serve as a deacon or elder of our church, convinced that our churches could use more business-savvy leadership. Regardless, Jesus calls such persons fools. Remember, this is the same Jesus who in Matthew 5:22 tells us not to call anyone a fool lest we be answerable by hell's fire! By the use of such strong language, Jesus castigates the person whom our present society elevates. In order to reconcile Jesus' harsh judgment with our capitalist social location, we must spiritualize the parable, interpreting it so that the sin is not hoarding resources that could be shared with those who had none but rather is relying on the individual to succeed instead of God. This metaphoric reading reinterprets the action of hoarding as the core of the sin and reduces it to the individual motivation of the person.

But those who read the Bible literally, those who live on the margins of society, instead agree with Jesus' pronouncement that this rich person is a fool. There exists the realization that those who hoard their profits usually believe that they have earned their wealth and thus are entitled to their riches and beholden to no one. This is what makes them fools. Missing from this analysis, however, is how societal privilege opens doors to one ethnic group at the expense of other groups.

I recall a student who insisted that his father's economic success, his rags-to-riches testimony, was due solely to his entrepreneurial skills. I simply asked one question: If his father were a black Latino, would he have been able to achieve the same level of success? Would he have had access to adequate public education, normally available in white suburban neighborhoods? Would he have been hired by his company for a managerial position? If hired, how many people on the margins would end up working in top administrative posts in the company, or would his color or ethnicity prevent him from passing the glass ceiling? Would he have gotten the necessary funding from the local bank to set out on his own? The student was forced to recognize that whiteness provided a privilege that contributed directly or indirectly to his father's success. If his father stores his profit believing that he has pulled himself up by his bootstraps, like the fool in Jesus' parable, the day will come when he will have to give an account for himself. He will have to reckon with his complicity with societal structures designed to privilege him at the expense of others whose skin pigmentation or ethnic background deprive them of the opportunities taken for granted by the dominant culture.

A HISPANIC CHRIST

José was a simple man who worked with his hands. He built things. He tried to make a living as a carpenter, but times were hard and taxes were high. Regardless of the foreign military occupation of his homeland, there simply was no time for him to become involved with any of those revolutionary groups doing maneuvers and hiding in the wilderness. He just worked hard, barely keeping food on the table for his rapidly growing family. Although a newlywed for less than nine months, his wife María had already given birth to his first child, a healthy boy. On this particular night, José was scared. He ran through the sleeping town, silently making his way toward his makeshift home, praying and hoping that he wasn't too late. He had to save his family from certain death! He burst into his shack and went straight to the sleeping mats on the dirt floor. "*Despierta mi amor*, wake up my love," José told his wife as he gently shook her. "A messenger just warned me that *la milicia*, the militia, will be coming for us. I fear we will disappear! *Apúrate*, hurry up, we must leave this moment for a safer land, far from the reaches of this brutal dictatorship." There was no time to pack any belongings or personal mementoes, nor was there time to say goodbye to friends and family. In the middle of the night, literally a few steps before the National Guard, José took his small family into *el exilio*, exile. They would come to a foreign country, wearing only the clothes on their backs. Even though they could not speak the language nor understand the strange customs and idiosyncracies of the dominant culture, at least they were physically safe. Salvation for this poor family was found *south* of the border.

Over two thousand years ago this family arrived in Egypt as political refugees, fleeing the tyrannical regime of Herod. Over forty years ago my own father came home to his wife, my mother, with similar news. Because of his involvement with the former political regime, he was now a fugitive of the newly installed government. If caught, he would face certain death. They gathered me, their six-month-old son, and headed north, arriving in this country literally with only the clothes on their backs. Like Jesus, I too was a political refugee, a victim of circumstances beyond my comprehension or control. My Jesus knows my pain of being a foreigner in an alien land. Jesus understands what it means to be seen as inferior because he too was from a culture different from the dominant one. I have no doubt that Jesus wept as a child for the same reasons I did. For me to see Jesus as a refugee is more than to locate my story in the biblical narrative. Rather, the story of Jesus becomes my story as I move from my social location to the biblical text. In short, I discover a Savior who knows the fears and frustrations of a small alien boy because Jesus also experienced those same fears and frustrations.

Latino/as, even though they have lived for hundreds of years on the land that would eventually become the United States, are still seen as aliens, exiles, and outsiders—people who are marginalized because they are perceived as not belonging. Many find themselves in the United States because of the quasi-religious ideology of Manifest Destiny, when the United States conquered foreign lands, as in the case of northern Mexico and Puerto Rico. The presence of these Mexicans and Puerto Ricans in the United States is a direct consequence of this country's aggressive territorial expansion. They awoke one day to find that the borders had moved, making them aliens on their own lands. Others are here as a result of gunboat diplomacy, as in the case of people from Central America and the Caribbean. During the twentieth century, many countries were invaded at least once by the U.S. Marines, whose mission usually involved overthrowing the country's government (even when elected by the people) to impose a government more willing to protect U.S. interests. For example, bananas were unknown in the United States prior to the twentieth century; yet by the early 1900s they were a common commodity. U.S. businesses established large plantations throughout Central and South America and used the U.S. Marines to establish puppet governments committed to protect U.S. trade, hence the term "banana republic." Territorial invasions and the exploitation of the natural resources by U.S. corporations led to conditions that eventually fostered the people's immigration to the imperial center. They find themselves as refugees and aliens in the country responsible for their being here. Even their descendants are not spared the indignation of being seen as foreigners, regardless of how many generations have inhabited the land. Their Latino/a physical features or Hispanic surnames make them a race that doesn't belong. For this reason, many anglicize their names to belong, a process familiar to Saul of Tarsus.

Many Euroamericans have heard eloquent sermons on how Saul, the persecutor of Christians, met Jesus on the road to Damascus, only to be converted to Paul the apostle. Saul's spiritual conversion led to a name change. While a charming interpretation, it ignores what the Bible actually says. After his encounter with the living Christ, the text goes on to say that Saul was converted and went to Jerusalem, where he met Barnabas and the twelve apostles. Saul went to Tarsus and Antioch, became a church leader, and then set out on his first missionary journey. In other words, Saul was a Christian. It is when Saul begins his missionary ventures that the book of Acts begins to refer to Saul as Paul. Saul, like so many Latino/as, had two names. One was used within his own culture, Saul the Jew, and one he used in the dominant culture, Paul the Roman citizen. Saul doesn't become Paul because of spiritual conversion; rather Saul *is* Paul, a product of a cultural *mestizaje*, a mixing together (Acts 8–9, 11, 13).[5]

Latina/os, like Saul/Paul, are viewed as a "half-breed" people. They are not considered pure members of the dominant culture because of their racial mixture, *mestizaje*. Hispanics are products of Iberian Europe, Native America, Africa, Asia, and, because of their presence in this country, North America. The mark of being Latina/o is a *mestizaje* that makes U.S. Hispanics heirs to several cultures yet seldom trusted or accepted by any of them—perpetual insiders and outsiders of five continents. The perceived stain of *mestizaje* makes Latino/as an object of disdain to the race-conscious dominant culture. The process of *mestizaje* began when the Spaniards conquered the Western Hemisphere. *Mestizos*, the offspring of the natural miscegenation that followed, became a pejorative term used toward people who fall short of the white ideal. Laws were passed to limit the mixture of races lest it undermine the barriers erected to separate "superior" cultures from "inferior" ones.[6] This mixture of cultures is not limited to the European conquest of the Americas. It continues when the mixed products of that violent clash attempt to define themselves within the United States.

Jesus' ethnic purity was also suspect as his contemporaries questioned his "legitimacy." A controversy within the early Christian church revolved around the *mestizaje* of Jesus. Jesus was accused of being the bastard child of the Jew Mary and a Roman soldier named Panthera. The title Jesus ben Panthera (Jesus son of Panthera) is not uncommon in rabbinical writings. The third-century theologian Origen makes a reference to this gossip when he writes,

Let us return, to the words put into the mouth of the Jew, where the mother of Jesus is described as having been turned out by the carpenter who was betrothed to her, as she had been convicted of adultery and had a child by a certain soldier named Panthera.[7]

The hint of impurity was sufficient grounds for excluding an individual from the congregation. According to Deuteronomy: "A bastard shall not enter the congregation of the Lord; even to his tenth generation shall he not enter into the Lord's congregation" (23:2). Religious leaders simply could not be suspected of *mestizaje*.

While I am not questioning the doctrine of the virgin birth, it is clear that many, specifically those who rejected Jesus' claim of messiahship, also rejected the claim that Mary gave birth to him while still a virgin. The real issue is that the gossip concerning Jesus' father made Jesus impure in the eyes of the "pure" Jewish race. If racial mixture for them meant impurity, then Jesus knew the pain and humiliation of being seen constantly as less than human because he was rumored to be biracial.

AN AMERINDIAN CHRIST

As the Amerindians of the Caribbean islands faced extinction, a missionary priest named Bartolomé de Las Casas attempted to defend the indigenous population from the European onslaught. Called to be a witness of Christ to the "godless" Amerindians, he realized that it was he who was living without God. For Las Casas, spiritual salvation was equated with the establishment of social justice, thereby inverting the relationship between the "Christ-bearing" Europeans and the "demonic" Amerindian heathens. It was the Spaniards who risked losing salvation because of their unjust treatment of the native population. Conversion for him ceased to be a simple profession of faith; rather conversion became an act or process by which one came to know Christ through seeking solidarity with the marginalized. This led him to write, "I leave in the Indies Jesus Christ, our God, scourged and afflicted and beaten and crucified not once, but thousands of times, when the Spaniards devastated and destroyed its people."[8] Over 450 years later, during the 1989 visit of Pope John Paul II to the Shrine of the Canadian Martyrs in Midland, Ontario, the Pope concluded his remarks by stating, "Not only is Christianity relevant to the Indian peoples, but Christ, in the members of his body, is himself Indian."[9]

The invading Europeans are not the ones who brought Christ to the so-called New World because Christ was already there. For both Las Casas and Pope John Paul II, Christ could be found among Amerindians, partly because of the oppression they suffer. Jesus Christ exists among an indigenous people who have historically been scourged by those wanting their land. Native American Christians believe that the Amerindian Christ reveals himself in the brokenness and suffering of all Amerindians who are lost between the world of their traditional habitat, from which they were separated by the Europeans, and Western culture. Amerindian Christians seek to find harmony between the biblical text, the teachings of Jesus, and the traditional wisdom of their elders.[10] These Christian Amerindians insist that if we want to find Christ, we need to look into the faces of the people that were systematically decimated. But *how* could Amerindians have Christ among them before they heard the story of Jesus?

In Acts 17:16–34, Paul encountered an altar in Athens with the inscription "TO THE UNKNOWN GOD." He addressed the Athenians, stating that he had come to introduce them to this God whom they worship but do not yet know. Paul explained that because God created the world and all that is within it, God is Lord of all the earth and does not reside in any temple or church made by human hands. Because this Creator "made every nation of one blood to dwell on all the face of the earth," God determined the bounds and time for their habitation. Hence, all people should "seek the Lord if perhaps they may feel God and find God, for God is never far from any one person." In God all humanity lives, moves, and has its being, and at the appointed time, God will bring people to a fuller revelation of Godself. Like the Athenians, Amerindians knew God prior to learning God's name, because Christ is for all people, incarnated in the history and religious ceremonies of the indigenous people. For example, among the Montagnais Nations located in Canada, the Amerindian Christ is a Christ who comes to save all people who open their hearts to Jesus. The elders would say that before they knew the God of Jesus Christ, they nevertheless prayed to this God, for God had already revealed

Godself to the Amerindians prior to the arrival of the white race. The Amerindians may not have yet recognized the importance of the cross or baptism, but regardless God, the Creator of all, was still guiding them.

In spite of God's movement among the Amerindians, Christian missionaries attempted to "Christianize the heathens." Even when done with the best of intentions, their religious endeavors contributed to the oppression of the indigenous people and eventually led to their downfall. It is important to recognize that those who brought the gospel to the Amerindians did so at a terrible cost to the indigenous population. Individuals like Las Casas or Henry Benjamin Whipple (a Catholic and a Protestant), who were heralded as defenders of the Indians, still contributed to their ultimate annihilation, in spite of their heartfelt convictions and intentions. Las Casas was responsible for creating the "reduction" paradigm for missionary conquest, which physically separated Amerindians from their families and communities, forcing them to live on the mission compound under the spiritual (and political) tutelage of the civilized Europeans. Whipple engineered the stealing of the Black Hills from the Sioux nation, thus bringing an end to their resistance. While these Christians may deserve recognition for criticizing the genocidal sins of the dominant culture, they also deserve condemnation for their tacit assumption that European white society was superior to that of the indigenous people. Regardless of their good intentions toward the welfare of the Amerindians, they, along with most missionaries to the Amerindian nations, failed to question how they fused and confused the message of the Bible with the values of their European culture, a blindness that led to the cultural genocide of those they hoped to defend.[11]

Cultural genocide of Amerindian life is as catastrophic to the people as military eradication, yet less perceptible. Whether intentionally or not, cultural genocide eradicates the integrity and worth of a people, an integrity and worth that served as the basis for their value system and their identity.[12] When ceremonial religious rituals were outlawed, like the Hopi Snake Dance or the plains Sun Dance, or when a warrior's conversion to Christ was measured by the length of his hair, then the imposition of the white Christ as defined by Euroamerican society led to the death of a people's soul and the obliteration of a people's culture.

"Without vision, my people perish," warns the prophet Hosea (4:6). As cultural genocide destroys the vision of a people, it turns them into nonpersons. The destruction of Amerindian life was not limited to the original conquest, which caused physical death. Many Amerindians who physically survived learned to view themselves as second-class citizens who *deserved* to occupy the bottom rungs of society's economic ladder. Powerless and dispossessed of their ancestral lands, Amerindians lost their identity as many began to see themselves in the way those from the dominant culture saw them. This process, which is not limited to the Amerindian experience, leads the marginalized group to internalize the illusion of inferiority constructed by the dominant culture while idealizing the white culture and its religious manifestations (including how it reads the Bible). This process of internalization usually leads toward self-hatred and the self-imposition of oppressive structures. While some Amerindians reject the message of liberation found in the Gospels, due mostly to how the symbol of the white Jesus continues to be linked to the death of their culture and ancestors, others are rediscovering the ways of their ancestors, learning to worship Jesus through their own cultural symbols.

For example, a present-day medicine man sees his work and that of Jesus to be similar in their attitude toward evil. When evil is given importance, it increases. Jesus teaches that when confronted, evil should be left to God, who can always be trusted and will never lose. Healing ceases to be simply physical. It also becomes a spiritual and psychological process that leads toward harmony. Both Jesus and the medicine man teach that the most important thing to learn from evil is that the beauty of life rests in living in harmony with God through brother Jesus who shows God's goodness.[13]

AN ASIAN AMERICAN CHRIST

The Christ originally introduced to the Asian community was a Christ understood through a culture defined by a Western ethos. The avarice of the West to colonize the "exotic" lands of the East created a Christ and a biblical understanding steeped in the imperialist and colonialist mind-set. A biblical rendering that assumes and demonstrates a European superiority creates a Christ who is complicit with the colonialist venture, a Christ responsible for justifying political structures that cause misery and death. For Christ to be Asian or Asian American, he, along with the Bible, must first be "decolonialized."

A colonialized Bible tends to romanticize the plight of the poor, even to the point of making the condition of the oppressed the model for the victims of racism, classism, and sexism. In Mark 12:41–44 (repeated in Luke 21:1–4) we are told the story of a poor widow who gives all that she has to the Temple.

> Sitting opposite the [Temple's] treasury, Jesus watched how the crowd cast copper coins into the treasury. Many rich people cast in much, but one poor widow came and cast two lepta, which is a quadrans. Having called his disciples close to him, Jesus said, "Truly I say to you that this poor widow cast more than all those casting into the treasury. For all cast out of their abundance, but she out of her poverty cast all, as much as she had, her whole livelihood."

The widow is generally idealized by the dominant culture as an example of Christian behavior for those who are poor, with her self-sacrifice compared with that of the self-indulgence of the religious leaders.

Yet, for some Asian Americans, this interpretation maintains societal power relationships that are detrimental to the oppressed. In Mark's account, the story of the widow's offering is preceded by Jesus' outrage toward the religious leaders who devour the possessions of widows. Mark states, "And [Jesus] said to them, . . . [the religious leaders are] devouring the houses of the widows under the pretense of praying at length" (12:38–40). In Luke's account, Jesus concludes the story of the widow's offering with his prediction of the Temple's destruction. Luke states, "Some were speaking about the Temple, that it was decorated with stones and gifts. He said, 'These things you see, days will come when one stone will not be left on a stone'" (21:5–6). Reading Mark and Luke together, we discover that Jesus is not praising the widow's offering as a paragon to be imitated by those who are marginalized; rather Jesus is denouncing a religious social structure that cons the widow out of the little she has.[14]

To side with the widows of the world becomes the appropriate action for *minjung*. *Minjung* is an untranslatable Korean word made up of two characters: *min*, which means "people," and *jung*, which means "mass." The word refers to all people who are marginalized and oppressed. When the poor are overburdened by economic structures designed to benefit the rich, then they belong to the *minjung*. When one race of people is dominated by another race so that the more powerful can extract cheap labor and resources, then they belong to the *minjung*. When one gender is domesticated by the other so as to serve the interests of those whom society says are the superior gender, then they belong to the *minjung*. *Minjung* theology is the theology of the colonized people, of those who are economically, politically, sexually, and socially oppressed. Jesus too belongs to the *minjung*, for throughout his earthly ministry he was followed by these masses of oppressed people; he ate with them, healed them, fed them, identified with them, and proclaimed God's liberation to them. A *minjung* reading of the Bible has its foundation in the life events of Jesus, events based not on power but powerlessness, events that sought justice for the disenfranchised. These events become the foundation for rereading the history of Asians and understanding what biblically based actions are required for liberation.[15]

A BLACK CHRIST

The only whites recorded in the Gospel story were the white colonizers from Rome. With certainty we can conclude that Jesus was not Aryan. Does this mean then that he belonged to another racial group or perhaps was black? For some black religious leaders like Albert Cleage, a Detroit pastor who ministers in a black ghetto church, Jesus' actual skin pigmentation was black. He was a black man who arose from the Black Nation of Israel. Cleage, along with some biblical scholars, insist that Jesus belonged to the nonwhite tribe of Judah, a mixture of different dark-skinned people groups who freely mixed with those of Africa. Hence Mary, Jesus' mother, was a black woman. Likewise, God is black. If God is Jesus' father, and if humans are created in the image of God, and if humans come in different colors, then these colors must find their source in God.

Now, if these different colors exist in God, then God cannot be white, based on how Euroamericans legally and socially define whiteness. By definition, according to Cleage, the son of a black God who was born to a black Mary is also black in the same way African Americans are defined as black in the United States. Cleage maintains that Jesus would not have been able to pass the "one-drop" rule, which defines blackness as having one drop of African blood flowing in your veins.

Other African American theologians, such as James Cone and J. Deotis Roberts, understand Christ's blackness as symbolic. For Cone, the inability of finite humans to capture the Infinite Being forces humans to use words as symbols, which always fall short in communicating the complete essence of the divine. A black Christ becomes the best way to represent Christ to African Americans struggling to survive in a racist society. Hence, Cone insists that Jesus' blackness is informed by his identification with the oppressed and despised people of the world, "the least of my people." Like Cone, Roberts also understands Jesus' blackness as symbolic. Yet, while Cone points to Jesus' blackness to emphasize Christ's particular relationship with African Americans, Roberts underscores Jesus' blackness to emphasize Christ's universal relationship with all of humanity. He attempts to meet a psychocultural need to claim self-worth for a people who are on their knees worshiping a Deity formed in the image of their historic oppressors. For Roberts, African Americans have a right to comprehend Jesus as black in the same way that white, red, yellow, and brown people have a right to comprehend Jesus in their own likeness. His call for a "universal" Christ will, he hopes, lead to long-lasting reconciliation among different people groups.

All three views agree that Jesus' blackness, whichever way that blackness is to be defined or envisioned, debunks blackness as something to be abhorred. Because the divine is black, Christ's identification with the struggle of African Americans is affirmed, and Christ's commitment to black liberation is emphasized.[16] To say that Jesus is black becomes more than promoting a notion that his ethnicity is of black origins. Skin color is *not* what is important. Jesus is black because blackness has historically been the color of oppression in this country; thus Christ's blackness is his ultimate expression of solidarity with marginality.

For all readers, the Scriptures are normally interpreted on the basis of the social location of the interpreter, in light of the interpreter's privilege or lack thereof. African Americans, more so than the dominant culture, identify with Jesus' humanity, specifically the communal aspects of the suffering Messiah, who suffered like so many African Americans did and do today. Jesus' birth, life, death, and resurrection become salvific motifs for the black experience. Yet this same Jesus, who willingly shares in the death-causing plight of the marginalized, also rose from the ultimate conclusion of oppression, death. This same Jesus is present in the lives of today's sufferers and will return to judge those who benefit from the unjust social structures that cause suffering. A black Christ thus stands in contrast to a white Christ and to a focus on the resurrection as "the beginning of a triumphalist church tradition that protects the status quo."[17]

A FEMALE CHRIST

In the previous chapter we reviewed how women in the Hebrew Bible were perceived as possessions who existed to meet the physical, emotional, economic, and sexual needs of men. They could be readily sacrificed for the sake of men's survival. Their ultimate function was to become vessels that carried the seeds of men. Hence the greatest shame a woman could ever bear was barrenness. This is evident in the story of Hannah as recorded in 1 Samuel 1. Because Hannah was barren, she was taunted by her husband's other wife. Bitter in her soul, she wept and refused to eat. She entered the Temple to ask for the only thing that would make her humanity whole, a man-child. Women find their fulfillment in life by the process of birthing great holy men (not women). If not, the shame of barrenness becomes so great that it leads women like Rachel, Jacob's wife, to exclaim in Genesis, "Give me sons, and if there are none, I shall die!" (30:2).

Good women are blessed with fertility. The so-called bad girls of the Bible are those who lacked the seriousness to be used by God to birth great men, heirs of God's promise. Even when women chose to break out of the restricted social space designated for them, as in the case of Mary of Magdala, we question their reputation. For example, what was Mary of Magdala's prior profession?

Did you say she was a prostitute? If you did, you are not alone. Yet nowhere in the Bible does it say Mary of Magdala was a prostitute. Where then did we get this idea?

According to all three Synoptic Gospels (Matt. 27:55–56; Mark 15:40–41; Luke 24:10), Mary of Magdala is mentioned first among Jesus' female disciples. Her role (along with other women) must have been important enough to be included as equal to the twelve male apostles. Luke states,

> Afterwards he traveled through every city and village, preaching and announcing the gospel of God's reign, and the twelve [apostles] were with him as well as certain women who were healed from evil spirits and infirmities: Mary being called Magdala from whom seven demons had gone out, and Joanna wife of Herod's steward Chuza, and Susanna, and many others who ministered to him from their possessions. (8:1–3)

In several apocryphal New Testament writings (e.g., the *Gospel of Philip*), Mary is characterized as an apostle who received revelations from the risen Christ. Contrary to tradition, which credits Peter as being the first witness of the resurrection (1 Cor. 15:4–6), Mary of Magdala was the first person to whom the risen Lord appeared and the first person to proclaim the Good News of the resurrection (Mark 16:9–10). In other writings, like the *Gospel of Mary,* she is referred to as the Apostle of the Apostles, for her rousing sermon to the despondent disciples after Christ's ascension.[18] No doubt, the biblical text and the early writings of the first church testify to the leadership position she held. Nonetheless, as the early Christian church reverted to patriarchal structures, the need arose to discredit Mary of Magdala so as to disqualify her position of authority within the church. Hence, the church tradition arose that she was a prostitute.

Mary of Magdala is not the only female leader of the Bible discredited by the early church's patriarchal hierarchy. John 4 tells the story of the Samaritan woman at the well. This woman has also been traditionally labeled a prostitute because she had five husbands and she was not married to the one she was presently with. She did not leave these men; she did not have the right. It was they who left her, and in a patriarchal society, she was in dire need of a new man who could provide for her basic survival needs. Although her situation was the result of the actions of these men and nowhere does the text state that she was a prostitute, we have been historically taught to characterize her as a harlot. Could it be because this is the first person to whom Jesus claims his messiahship, leading her to become the first citywide evangelist? Hence she too was discredited lest other women in the church use her as a model in claiming their spiritual calling to lead. After all, if the woman at the well and Mary of Magdala were prostitutes, how could they serve as paragons to emulate (although Jesus associated with prostitutes and promised his reign to them)?

Yet, in spite of this ingrained social bias toward women, Jesus attempted to debunk patriarchy. In Luke, we are told of an incident that involved two of Jesus' disciples, Martha and Mary:

> And in their travels it occurred that [Jesus] entered into a certain village. A certain woman by the name of Martha received him into her house. She had a sister named Mary who sat at the feet of Jesus to hear his words. But Martha was distracted with all the serving and said, "Lord, do you not care that my sister left me alone to serve? Tell her then that she should help me." Answering her, Jesus said, "Martha, Martha, you are anxious and troubled about many things when there is need of only one, and Mary chose the good part, which shall not be taken from her." (10:38–42)

Many sermons have been based on this text. For many, the main message is the need for believers not to worry about all the cares of this world (e.g., housework) as did Martha but, rather, to take the time to be with Jesus as did Mary. While such a message is uplifting, it falls short of uncovering the radical dismantling of a patriarchal system that was undertaken by Jesus. Through his actions, he denounced the assumption that women had no place in religious life. In fact, according to the wisdom of the time, if there was only one Torah left in the world and it fell into the hands of a woman to care for, it would have been better that the Torah be destroyed than have a woman touch it. This type of attitude led pious Jewish men to begin their morning prayers thanking God that God did not make them a Gentile, a slave, or a woman.

Did this attitude toward women influence how women are remembered by the male writers of the Gospels? The text indicates that Martha was distracted by her serving duties. The Greek word Luke uses in the text for serving is *diakonia*. Nowhere in Luke's story does it tell us that Martha was serving in the kitchen doing "woman's work," which is how this narrative is usually interpreted. Her duties in serving, more than likely, corresponded with the office of church deacon established in Acts 6:1–6. Luke (who also authored Acts) indicates that among the first deacons of the church (if not the first), upon which future ones would be modeled, is this woman. Martha's preoccupation with serving dealt with her duties and responsibilities toward the house-church that met at her home, leaving her little time to also "sit at Jesus' feet."

Mary is also a disciple who serves and proclaims God's message, but on this day she chose "to sit at Jesus' feet." The Bible is not interested in telling us that there were no chairs available in the room, so Mary was left sitting on the floor. Rather, to study at the feet of a teacher was a euphemism indicating that the person who is sitting is the student or disciple of a master, a role reserved for men. For example, in Acts 22:3 the same phrase describes Paul's relation to his teacher Gamaliel. The text says Paul studied "at the feet of Gamaliel." Hence, Mary not only touched Torah; she also read and studied it! Furthermore, these two sisters are portrayed in the Gospel of John as well-known apostolic figures of the early church who were beloved by Christ (11:5). Parallel to Peter's confession of Jesus' messiahship (Matt. 16:15–19), Martha also served as a spokesperson for the early church according to John 11:27. Additionally, through Mary's evangelism, many came to believe in Jesus (John 11:45).[19] These women were hearers, servers, and proclaimers of the word.

Let's now reread the story through the eyes of women. The rabbi Jesus was received in the home of one of his apostles named Martha, who also served as founder and deacon of the house-church in Bethany where she proclaimed God's word. On this day her sister Mary the evangelist sat at the feet of Jesus to study Torah. Martha asked the rabbi to have his student help with the duties required by the deacon, but the rabbi responded that studying Torah was just as important as serving.

The radicalness of this narrative affirms leadership positions assumed by women during Jesus' earthly ministries, even though it was considered blasphemous by the more legalistic religious leaders of his time. Such a reading should not lead the reader to assume that Christianity's treatment of women was more liberating than the Jewish treatment of women, only that Jesus' actions attempted to dismantle patriarchal structures. However, the men who led the post-Pentecost Christian church were quick to forget Jesus' example and reverted to patriarchal models.

Regardless of how we interpret Jesus' solidarity with women, for several feminists, as long as Christ remains a male, it is difficult for women to find a Savior who has experienced the trials and tribulations distinctive to women. What then does it mean to have a female Christ? This does not imply an androgynous Christ, for Jesus was born male, with masculine sexual organs. What is meant by a female Christ is that he was symbolically female. In the same way that we can talk about an economically marginalized Christ, a Hispanic Christ, an Amerindian Christ, an Asian American Christ, and a black Christ, we can also talk about a female Christ. But is Jesus' symbolic femaleness enough? For some feminist theologians, like Mary Daly, the maleness attached to Jesus makes the problem of finding salvation in a male Savior overwhelming.[20] Other feminist scholars, like Rosemary Ruether, insist that in spite of Jesus' male gender, he stood against all forms of hierarchal systems that privileged one group at the expense of another. These systems include patriarchal structures.[21] Because Jesus continues to be incarnated among "the least of my people," Jesus is a woman. He can be understood as being female because there is no distinction between male and female in Christ and because at times he referred to the Deity's characteristics in the feminine.

First, Jesus can be perceived in the feminine because the biblical text teaches that in Christ there is no male or female. The preoccupation with making the male perspective the central lens by which Christ is identified and understood prevents the inclusiveness of Christ that Paul calls for in Galatians, where he turns the morning Jewish prayer of thanksgiving mentioned above on its head: "For as many as were baptized in Christ, you put on Christ, so there is no Jew or Gentile, slave or free, male or female, for you are all one in Christ" (3:27–28). When Paul calls the church to form one body in Christ, that body is composed of both males and females who participate in the living, dying, and resurrection of Christ. This participation, not the replication of sexual features, becomes the model for Christ's image.

In Acts 9:1–5 Saul was traveling to Damascus to persecute the early Christian church when he was blinded by a light that knocked him to the ground. He heard a voice asking, "Saul, Saul, why are you persecuting me?" This narrative begins by informing the reader of Saul's motive for going to Damascus, to arrest followers of the early church. The text specifically states that Saul was looking for "men or women" to persecute. So, when Saul asks who it is that he is persecuting, the response is, "I am Jesus, and you are persecuting me." This passage clearly teaches that Jesus is the persecuted church, male and female, without distinction. Historically, Jesus may be male, but his sacramental identification with the persecuted makes them identical with Christ. If, however, Jesus' historical maleness is interpreted as essential to his deistic identity and redemptive functions, then Christ is religiously construed to marginalize women.[22]

Jesus can also be viewed as female because a feminine image of the Deity appears in several places throughout the Bible. Humans can never fathom the total mystery of the Deity. There exists no symbol, word, concept, or idea perceivable by humans that totally encompasses the essence of God. The best we can do is to describe the Deity in human-constructed words that fall short of completely and thoroughly describing that which no mind can totally comprehend. Hence we say God is a consuming fire, God is a vineyard owner, or God is a father. While these words are insufficient to describe God, they do provide a glimpse into the eternal Creator. Likewise, there exist feminine words and symbols that the Bible uses to describe the Deity. For example, in Isaiah, the prophet writes, "I [God] have forever kept silence. I was quiet and refrained myself. I will groan like a woman in labor, I will pant and I will gasp" (42:14).[23] Jesus picks up this imagery and refers to the other two members of the Trinity in the feminine. Of the Spirit, Jesus says in John 3:6 that to be a Christian, one must emerge from the Spirit's womb, that is, be "born again." The Spirit, like a woman in labor, gives birth to those who become new creatures in Christ. When speaking about God's mercy in Luke 15, Jesus likens God to the father of a prodigal son, a shepherd who lost one sheep, and a woman who has lost her coin. God is Father, God is Shepherd, God is Woman.

Again, as mentioned in chapter 4, God is beyond gender. For this reason, Pope John Paul I was able to proclaim, "We know [God] always has his eyes open on us, even when it seems to be dark. God is our father; even more God is our mother."[24] Nevertheless, many feminist theologians have raised concerns about praising the Deity's feminine side by idealizing a romantic notion of motherhood. If "mother" becomes the only attribute projected upon the Deity, then a patriarchal ideology is maintained, where being a woman is reduced to bearing and rearing children.

In addition to the concerns raised by some feminist scholars, some black feminists, better known as "womanists," insist that their white counterparts have not seriously considered the dimensions of racism (and classism) within the women's movement. White feminists' goals and objectives do not always consider the needs of African American women. Likewise, a theological understanding of Christ is different when considered from within the black community.

For womanists like Jacquelyn Grant, five experiences grounded in the black woman's social location demonstrate how Jesus can be liberated from the patriarchy, white supremacy, and economic privilege that imprison Christ. First, Jesus is a cosufferer because he made an option to suffer with the marginalized of his time. Second, Jesus is an equalizer because he came for all humanity. Third, Jesus initiates freedom, remembering that freedom is not defined as becoming equal to the oppressor (what womanists claim white feminists are doing) but as liberation from the oppressor for the women and men of the black community. Fourth, Jesus is the sustainer, a model for the family that has been systematically violated due to slavery and its aftermath. And finally, fifth, Jesus is the liberator because his liberative activities during his earthly ministry empower black women in their own quest for liberation.[25]

For some Asian feminists, Jesus is the compassionate mother, bearing the sins and suffering of everyone, making him the ultimate symbol for oppressed women on the margins. In some Asian cultures, such as Korea, shamans who liberate people from *han* (the feeling of resentment, helplessness, bitterness, sorrow, and revenge felt deep in the victim's guts) tend to be women. Hence,

Jesus, the compassionate mother, willingly bears the sufferings of the *minjung* and symbolically participates in the feminine activity of healing the *han* of the *minjung*. In Jesus, suffering women identify with the suffering of Jesus not to glorify suffering but rather to find a Deity who understands the pain of oppression and is willing to become one with the sufferer. Jesus weeps and cries out in pain, like so many Asian women who have lost their sons and daughters to foreign Western military aggression or national secret police agencies. When Jesus cried out for Jerusalem in Matthew 23:37, his *han* was so deep that the Gospel writer uses a feminine metaphor, having Jesus refer to himself as a mother hen attempting to gather her brood under her protective wing.[26]

A GAY CHRIST

On October 6, 1998, in the small Wyoming city of Laramie, a twenty-one-year-old college freshman majoring in political science, named Matthew Shepard, entered the Fireside Bar for a Heineken. He entered the bar alone around ten o'clock, coming from a dinner meeting with friends from the Lesbian, Gay, Bisexual, and Transgendered Alliance. There he met two individuals to whom Shepard revealed his homosexuality. The two individuals said that they too were gay and invited Shepard to leave with them. A little after midnight, they piled into a pickup truck and Shepard's assault began. He was later found pistol-whipped with a .357 magnum and left for dead, strung up on a split-rail fence along an old dirt road. He died several days later, never recovering from a coma.

During the memorial service, bomb-sniffing dogs combed the church while SWAT teams and police in riot helmets were needed to keep the peace. Anti-gay protestors from different churches chose Shepard's funeral to protest what they perceived to be too much tolerance and too many concessions to the gay community. "We want to inject a little sanity and Gospel truth into what is shaping up to be an orgy of homosexual lies and propaganda" said the Reverend Fred Phelps, a Baptist preacher from Topeka, Kansas, who came with several members of his congregation to protest the memorial service. These church members waved antigay signs, shouted anti-gay slogans, and engaged mourners in loud and nasty debates. One protestor yelled, "Matthew was wicked!" Some of the signs read, "No Fags in Heaven," "God Hates Fags," and "No Tears for Queers." One young girl, too young to even understand the message she held, carried a sign that read, "Fag = Anal Sex."[27]

No doubt, many within the overall Christian church have strong negative attitudes toward gays and lesbians. Some Christians encourage violence toward gays and lesbians when they reduce sexual orientation to a disease or sin and encourage a crusade against those whom they perceive God hates. Violence is further advocated when Christians remain silent in the face of the violence experienced by the Shepards of our community. Perpetrators of gay bashing feel themselves justified in enforcing the rules of God and nature, administering justice to those whom God hates. Christians become complicit with the violence they breed due to their attitudes, words, and actions toward "the least of my people."

Historically, biblical texts have been used as clubs to submit gays and lesbians to conformity. Some of the most verbal (and physical) attacks upon gays and lesbians have been generated from the conservative Christian community, as demonstrated during Shepard's funeral. Yet Jesus warns that anyone who calls someone *rhaka* will be liable to the Sanhedrin or even hell's fire (Matt. 5:22). Most Bibles translate the Aramaic term *rhaka* as "fool" or renegade; however, scholars have suggested that the word could also be translated as "sissy."[28] Regardless, Jesus clearly indicates that the many Christians who participate in name-calling are in danger of condemnation. Why? Because all of God's creatures contain the image of God, all have dignity and worth, and all, as part of the creation story, participate in the final words of the sixth day of creation, "And God saw all which God had made, and behold, it was very good" (Gen. 1:31). Gays and lesbians, known by God before they were formed in their mother's womb (Jer. 1:5), are also part of God's creation, and hence, they too are good.

Because of the violence many gays and lesbians face, they must also be considered among "the least of my people." The social pressure to conform to heterosexuality, the tormented experience of an orientation that contrasts with what society considers normative, and the physical danger encountered as hate crimes and gay bashing continue to rise in this nation relegate gays and lesbians to the margins of society. If we say that Jesus is in solidarity with "the least of my people" and if gays find themselves the victims of oppressive acts, then we must conclude that, to remain faithful to a liberative reading of the Bible, Jesus is gay, not because he has participated in homosexual activities but because what is done to the "the least of my people" is done to Christ. When Matthew Shepard was crucified, Jesus was again crucified.

In Matthew 19:10–12 Jesus proclaims his own celibacy, indicating that he did not partake in any sexual activity; however, for a person who chooses celibacy as a way of glorifying God, sexuality can become a sinful temptation, whether it be heterosexual or homosexual. If this is true, then Hebrews assumes a deeper meaning when it states, "We have one [Jesus] who has been tempted in *every way* that we have, although he is without sin" (4:15). If Jesus was tempted in *every way,* then we must consider that he was tempted with both heterosexuality and homosexuality. Nonetheless, Jesus' gayness is not due to sexuality but to solidarity.

PERCEIVING THE CHARACTER OF DIVINITY

Jesus Christ is the fullest revelation of God to humanity. Not only do we mere humans learn the character of God; through Christ, God learns what it means to suffer under oppression. Because the ultimate Deity has flesh wounds upon its hands, feet, and side, God understands the pain and suffering of all who also face persecution. The disenfranchised can pray to God about their marginalized existence because God's very incarnation made God one with those who have always been crucified by society. To read the Bible cognizant that Jesus Christ suffered marginality is to rebel against the assumption of the Euroamerican church that the task of all Bible readers is to discover the one single interpretation of the text, which by definition becomes the interpretation of the dominant culture. To read the Bible from the margins debunks these interpretations and unmasks how they have been used historically to justify the power and privilege of the few at the expense of the many.

While the dominant culture may debate the existence of God, people of the margins attempt to ascertain the character of God. Jesus Christ becomes the point of departure in discerning God's character. While the Bible provides crucial revelations of

God's character, we must remember that the Bible is not God. To assert the biblical text as divine borders on heresy in the same way that the Israelites confused the raised bronzed serpent with God.[29] The purpose of the Bible is to give testimony to Christ's liberative and salvific message. The Bible does not save, only God can. This does not minimize or cheapen the importance of the biblical text; it only puts it in its proper relationship to Jesus Christ, by whom we can behold the character of God.

God Sides with Today's Crucified People

I have two children, a ten-year-old boy and a nine-year-old girl. I love both children deeply and would gladly lay down my life for either one of them. Yet they do one thing that drives me crazy. They love to fight, and not a day goes by that they are not arguing over something trivial. Now, my son is about a foot taller than my daughter, a year older, and a bit stronger. When their verbal fights become physical, my son has the clear advantage. He can easily pin her to the ground and use the privilege of his gender and height to win the confrontation. When I see them physically fighting, I step in, pick him up by the nap of his neck, and defend my daughter. Imagine if my son would look at me and say, "Wait a minute, father, you are being unfair. You are choosing sides; specifically, you are choosing her side. As a father who loves us equally, you should not take sides; it is simply unfair." You can imagine my response, "I love you dearly, and my taking her side does not mean I love you any less. However, I will side with the one being abused. I will side with the one being oppressed. Not because I love her more but because she is being oppressed, even if it means that I take a stand against you."

Likewise, Christ sides with those who are being oppressed, those who are today's crucified. This means that Christ takes a stand against those who are oppressing them, that is, those from the dominant culture who, due to unwarranted power and privilege, benefit at the expense of the powerless. Christ stands against oppression and compels his followers to do likewise. Christ resides among those who are suffering oppression, who live in want, who have misery as a companion. These are the "the least of my people," Jesus in the here and now. The poor, the oppressed, and people of color provide an essential salvific perspective to world history. God chooses those who are oppressed within history and makes them the principal means of salvation for the rest of society, just as God chose the "suffering servant," the crucified Christ, to bring salvation to the world.

For now, suffice to say that God has historically chosen those from the margins of society to be agents of God's new creation. As Matthew 21:42 reminds us, it is the stone rejected by the builders that becomes the keystone of God's handiwork. God did not reveal the divine will to the court of Pharaoh; instead, God chose their slaves, the Hebrews, to reveal God's movement in history. It was not Rome, the most powerful city of the known world, where God chose to perform the miracle of the incarnation, nor was it Jerusalem, the center of Yahweh worship; rather it was impoverished Galilee. This theme of solidarity between the crucified Christ and the victims of oppression makes the people of the margins salvific agents for the recipients of society's power and privilege.

Christ is informed by the historical identification of Jesus with those who suffer under oppression. Christ's nonwhiteness is not due to an attempt to be "politically correct," nor to some psychological need of marginalized communities. Jesus is nonwhite because the biblical witness of God is of one who takes sides with those who are oppressed against their oppressors. In our present racist society, people of color are the ones being oppressed, the ones who suffer hunger, thirst, nakedness, alienation, affliction, and incarceration.

In a new world order, for those who are the wretched of the land, Christ ceases to be a religious icon, located somewhere far away in the heavens, who simply listens to prayers begging for blessings or to unanswerable questions about the injustices that accompany humanity. To be an imitator of Christ is to learn how to share each other's pains, to share each other's sufferings, and together share those pains and sufferings with the one who reminds us of the trials and tribulations of this world yet encourages us to be of good cheer, for the world has been overcome through the power of love, manifested in physical deeds of solidarity with "the least of my people." A Christ who does not call us to build God's reign of justice or to seek liberation from all forms of sins, regardless of the cost to our personhood, is a false Christ. Christians are called upon to show their love for one another, a love rooted in a willingness to lay down their lives for the very least who presently suffer under race, class, and gender oppression.

God Is Victorious

The life, death, and resurrection of Jesus Christ has taught us that God is foremost a liberator, not just from the narrow constraints of "personal sins" but also from the sins of the whole community that wreak havoc on the lives of those who reside on the margins of society. The resurrection of Jesus Christ on the third day after his crucifixion guarantees victory over the forces of darkness that are bent on imposing structures designed to benefit those with power at the expense of those without. The resurrection insures that while these structures that impose death and misery may appear to triumph in this world, in the end they will crumble. Second, the resurrection also guarantees that Christ is alive, present in this time and space, among the same people with whom he communed during his earthly ministry, "the least of my people." Thus, from the underside of history, where multitudes are forced to suffer under the yoke of domination, the quest to understand Christ becomes a quest for liberation, liberation from racism, classism, and sexism.

Because the experiences of those relegated to the margins of society closely resemble the lot of God's crucified people, their struggle for life and dignity becomes central in interpreting the Christ of the Gospels. To look at a Latino/a Christ, an Amerindian Christ, an Asian Christ, a black Christ, a female Christ, or even a gay Christ subverts the normative white Christ of power and privilege. Just as whites worship a Christ in their own image, it becomes significant to see the divine in the color of those who are oppressed. The white Christ of history has been the Christ who justified the historical reality of conquest, slavery, racism, numerous massacres, imperialism, and colonialism. It was in the name of the white Christ, the Christ who symbolized the protection of white Christian civilization, that atrocities against people on the margins were committed throughout history. For the dominant culture to see and know Jesus, it must search for him among God's crucified people, those most oppressed by structural racism, sexism, and classism. Only then can those with power and privilege find their salvation.

CHAPTER 6

Jesus Saves

Every semester, without fail, one of my students asks *the* litmus-test question by which most in my class assess my spirituality and my commitment to the Christian faith. The question simply is, "Do you have a personal relationship with Jesus Christ?" I habitually answer, "No, I have a public relationship with Jesus Christ." This response usually raises eyebrows as my students attempt to figure out what I mean. I hope that my insistence on stressing a "public relationship" instead of a "personal relationship" helps students realize how their question is a product of their generally Euroamerican culture, which shapes their theological understanding of the biblical text.

I attempt to elucidate my comment by telling them about a recent trip I took to Las Vegas. I relate that I took off my wedding ring, gave it to my wife for safekeeping, and told her that I wasn't going to wear it on my trip because we had a personal relationship. No public manifestation of that relationship is necessary to signify what is personal. You can imagine my wife's response! She reminded me that our relationship cannot be reduced to just the personal, for we also share a public, albeit intimate, relationship. The ring is not what makes me married; rather, my act of wearing a ring becomes an outward expression of an inward commitment. It becomes a symbol that publically signifies my faithfulness.

Likewise, my relationship with Jesus Christ is both public and intimate. As the ring is an outward expression of an inward commitment, so too do my actions (praxis) in establishing love and justice become outward expressions of my internal Christian commitment. My praxis becomes the symbolic wedding ring signifying my union with Christ. "By this everyone will know that you are my disciples: if you have love for one another," Jesus says in John 13:35. In fact, confining Jesus to my personal life becomes the ultimate act of religious selfishness. But then again individualism, guarding the private, is what's most celebrated and prized within the dominant U.S. culture.

Probably to a greater degree than in any other nation, hyperindividuality is a salient characteristic of the U.S. ethos. According to Robert Bellah's groundbreaking sociological work, the individualism commonly expressed in the Euroamerican culture is based on two at times contradictory notions: 1) a belief in the inherent dignity and sacredness of individuals; and 2) a belief in the primary reality of the individual, with society relegated to second place. Social, political, and religious relationships are conducted with the individual at the center. A type of Christianity develops that is private, emphasizing an individually constructed spiritual experience. Hence, it is possible to speak of 275 million religions within the United States, one for each person.[1] As the culture relegates its religious beliefs to a private matter, the danger that can arise is that a form of Christianity, devoid of social responsibility or action, can develop subjected to the general civil will. Eventually the collective goals of society fostered by this hyperindividuality can become interpreted as a religious mandate for all.

Yet Christianity is never private. Among the English-speaking dominant culture, to be private is something to be valued and guarded, reflecting the hyperindividuality of the Euroamerican milieu. Still, among those who speak Spanish, one way of defining the word "private," *privado,* is by its derivation from the word *privar,* "to deprive," from where we get the word *privación,* which is translated as both "deprivation" and "privacy." For the Hispanic, to be private is in fact to be deprived, deprived of family, of friends, or of community. For Latino/as, who stress a communal understanding of their relationship with Christ, terms such as "a personal relationship" can become antitheses to their cultural ethos.

If indeed theology reflects the cultural and philosophical milieu of a people, then we should not be surprised when a highly individualistic society imposes this characteristic on the biblical texts and reduces the human-divine relationship to a personal one. An example of this can be noted in the call to conversion made by Billy Graham, perhaps the best-known evangelist of the second half of the twentieth century. Dr. Graham writes,

If *you* are willing to repent for *your* sins and receive Jesus Christ as *your* Lord and Savior, *you* can do it now. At this moment *you* can . . . say this little prayer: O God, *I* acknowledge that *I* have sinned against You. *I* am sorry for *my* sins. *I* am willing to turn from *my* sins. *I* openly receive and acknowledge Jesus Christ as *my* Savior. *I* confess Him as Lord. From this moment on *I* want to live for Him and serve Him. In Jesus' name. Amen.[2]

The first thing that is obvious about this approach is that the relationship is centered on the individual. The individual is the agent of all the verbs used in the above-quoted invitation to become born again. The Deity is either the object of the verb or a possessive pronoun, to be possessed by the individual. Our own language betrays the way in which we place ourselves as the principal actor in the encounter between the individual and the divine. Also to be noted is that the emphasis is on the act of God in Jesus Christ as Savior. No attention is given to Jesus' human actions toward those who were marginalized during his time. Hence no connection is made concerning the obligation of converts toward those who are oppressed today. Those privileged by our social structures are free to continue their quest for power and riches without having to fear for their salvation, regardless of how it affects those who are marginalized.

This is not to minimize or negate the importance of a conversion experience for Christians who claim to have a relationship with Jesus Christ. The danger exists when salvation is reduced solely to an act where the individual makes the choice of accepting Jesus, as if the divine needs our acceptance or recognition to be a force in the lives of humans. One of the religious marks of a hyperindividualistic society is an emphasis on a personal relationship with God. At times, this evangelistic approach ignores the relationship between praxis and faith. Being a Christian is reduced to an issue of belief. Solely to believe in Jesus is sufficient for salvation. While belief is important, if not crucial, it alone is inadequate. This is made clear within the biblical text, as illustrated in the encounter Jesus had with three separate individuals seeking salvation.

THE RICH YOUNG RULER, THE SINNING TAX COLLECTOR, AND THE BEGGING BLIND MAN

Luke 18:18–30 tells of a young man, a member of a leading family, who approaches Jesus, asking the question "Good Master, what must I do to inherit eternal life?" As a former Southern Baptist pastor of a small rural Kentucky church, I used to live for questions like this and had no doubt as to my response. After leading the seeker through "Roman's road to salvation" outlined in Paul's letter to the Romans, I would guide them through a sinner's prayer (similar to the one in Dr. Graham's book); have them walk down the church aisle, make a public profession, and join the church; admonish them to give up drinking and carousing; and get them baptized the following Sunday. Depending on denominational association, this is how many ministers throughout the United States would have answered the question of the young man in Luke.

Fortunately, Jesus does not give this response. Jesus does not invite the young aristocrat to repent of his sins and then ask that he allow Jesus to enter into his life in a personal relationship. Instead, Jesus tells him to keep the commandments, which the rich young man confesses he has kept since his earliest days. Then Jesus does the unexpected. Rather than simply accept the young man as a follower, Jesus tells him to sell all that he owns and distribute the money to the poor so as to gain treasures in heaven. Then he can follow Jesus. But when the rich young man heard this, he became full of sadness.

As the rich young man walks away, Jesus makes a disturbing pronouncement: "How hard it is for those having riches to enter into the reign of God. For it is easier for a camel to go through an eye of a needle than for a rich person to enter into the reign of God" (18:24–25). It appears that for the rich, Jesus determines salvation by how they interact with the poor. It is important to note that the term "poor" does not just refer to a lack of financial resources; instead, "poor" encompasses the inequality and injustice that accompany the lack of access to opportunities that the dominant culture takes for granted as a privileged right.

Yet some readers will turn to Ephesians, which clearly states, "For by grace you are being saved, through faith, and this not of yourselves, it is a gift from God; not works, lest anyone should boast" (2:8–9). After all, Isaiah reminds us that "all of our righteous acts are like filthy rags" (64:6). How then can Jesus make the salvation of this rich young aristocrat conditional on his treatment of the poor? Often the dominant culture reconciles this apparent contradiction by employing a metaphoric reading. Such an interpretation recognizes the primary message of the story, which is that Jesus must be the center of every aspect of the life of the believer. All idols, whether they are riches *or something else,* status, family, ethnicity, and so on, must be relinquished. In this story, wealth just happens to be the idol of this young man. And his downfall was his unwillingness to abandon this particular idol. And the probable conclusion of the dominant culture is that the wealthy of today must also be willing to give up everything for Jesus but they don't *really* have to do it or radically change their lifestyles.

Yet, as previously discussed, the margins apply a different understanding; that is, they see Jesus literally connecting the salvation of the rich man with his response to the poor. Anyone who claims power and privilege, whether they come from maleness, whiteness, or economic class, forfeits his or her claim to God's eschatological promise, just like the rich young ruler. God's reign is not promised to those who are oppressors or benefit from oppressive structures. In fact, if they insist on their lifestyle, they have no place or claim to God's hope. In Luke 6:20–21 and 24–25, Jesus said that the poor are those who should be happy, for theirs is the reign of God. And what about those who do not produce the fruits Jesus sought in the life of the rich young ruler? Jesus says, "Already the axe is laid at the root of the trees; thus, any tree that does not produce good fruit is cut down and thrown into the fire" (Matt. 3:10). The internal salvific transformation caused by the grace of God is manifested publically by how the individual interacts with others, specifically those who are marginalized.

Believing in Jesus is insufficient for obtaining salvation. Does not the author of the letter of James warn us that even the demons believe in Jesus and tremble at his name?

> My brothers and sisters, what profits those who say they have faith but do not have works? Is faith able to save them? If a brother or sister is naked and lacking daily food, and any one

of you says, "Go in peace, be warmed and filled," but does
not give them the necessities of the body, what is the profit? So also faith, if it has no works, is dead by itself. Yet one
will say, "You have faith and I have works." Show me your
faith without your works and I will show you my faith by my
works. You believe God is one. You do well, but even the
demons believe and tremble. But are you willing to know,
O vain one, that faith without works is dead? . . . You see
then that by works a person is justified, and not by faith alone.
. . . For the body without spirit is dead, so also faith without
works is dead. (2:14–20, 24, 26)

Concentrating solely on personal faith in Jesus Christ, divorced
from actions of loving justice, encourages cheap grace. People from
the margins insist that Christians move beyond an abstract belief
in Jesus to a material response to those who are hungry, thirsty,
naked, alien, sick, and incarcerated. The task for those seeking eternal life must go beyond an intellectual understanding of Jesus
Christ to the actual doing of Christlike actions—not because salvation is achieved by those actions but because they serve as witness to the empowering grace given by God. To continue worshiping Christ apart from any commitment to those who are the
least contributes to maintaining our present structures of oppression along gender, race, and class lines. To ignore the cry of those
who are marginalized is to deny Christ's message, regardless of
whether or not we confess our belief in him and proclaim his name
with our lips.

While people on the margins often connect the responsibility
of those who benefit by the way society is structured with the
process of salvation, those accustomed to a privileged lifestyle usually dismiss such a theological perspective. A faith solely based on
individual belief and disconnected from public responsibilities and
actions allows the rich young rulers of our time to claim to be followers and disciples. If the words of Jesus are as true today as they
were two thousand years ago, then "how hard it is for those [of
the dominant culture] to enter into the reign of God. For it is easier for a camel to go through an eye of a needle than for [those of
the privileged center] to enter into the reign of God" (Luke
18:24–25).

More Than Just Climbing Sycamore Trees

It seems as if the author of Luke knew that readers would try to spiritualize the story of the rich young ruler. To counteract the attempt to harmonize the story of the rich young ruler with the lifestyle of today's wealthy, numerous homilies preached at prestigious congregations throughout this country have maintained that Jesus *really* did not mean to bind the salvation of the privileged with their actions toward the disenfranchised. Yet Luke 19:1–10 continues his Gospel by recounting the story of the rich sinner Zacchaeus.

According to Luke, Zacchaeus was a senior tax collector, a post that made him a very wealthy man. In the Roman Empire, contracts to collect taxes were farmed out to wealthy persons who in turn hired local residents, like Zacchaeus, to do the actual collecting of funds. These individuals became personally responsible for paying Rome its taxes, although they were provided with the power of Rome to collect extra taxes from the masses in order to make a profit. Theft and fraud abounded as tax collectors attempted to appropriate the maximum amount a person could bear. Their dealings with Gentiles made Jewish tax collectors ritually unclean, and their dealings with Rome made them collaborators with the occupying colonizers and traitors to their own people. While the rich young man was accepted by the people for his faithfulness in keeping the law of Moses and his membership in one of the leading families of the city, Zacchaeus was rejected because he did not keep the commandments and had unethically obtained his riches.

Consequently, Jesus surprised everyone, even Zacchaeus, when he stated that he would stay at his home. The crowd that surrounded Jesus began to complain, murmuring, "He is going to stay at a sinner's home." Zacchaeus, probably for the first time in his life, regained his humanity as Jesus accepted him. This internal empowering by God's grace was immediately manifested in his actions toward the poor. In 19:8 Zacchaeus exclaims, "Behold, half of my possessions I give to the poor, and if I cheated anyone, I restore it fourfold." How did Jesus respond? Jesus did not reassure him that this was not really necessary. Instead Jesus responded, "Today salvation has come to this house!" (19:9). Salvation

entered Zacchaeus' house when God's grace was manifested as
actions toward the poor, when Zacchaeus publicly died to the
power and privilege that had supported his lifestyle.

I Once Was Blind

Sandwiched between the story of the rich young ruler and the sinful tax collector is the short account of a poor blind man. This is
not the only time the author of Luke provides meaning to an overall narrative by sandwiching in its midst a short and seemingly unre-
lated event. We must remember that the texts that eventually
became part of the biblical canon did not have chapter number-
ing, verse breaks, or story headings when they were originally written. These were added afterwards. In other words, the end of Luke
18 does not signify a new and different story with the start of Luke
19. Instead, the story of two rich men, one acceptable to society
and the other despised by society, is one complete narrative that
serves to contrast the one liked but rejected by Christ with the one
whom the reader thought would never make it yet was accepted
by Christ. What separates these two men in their attainment of salvation? It seems to be their relationship and commitment, or lack
thereof, with and to the marginalized.

Sandwiched in the midst of their stories is a short account
(18:35–43) of a blind man begging by the side of the road. When
he heard the crowd approach, he asked what was going on. The
crowd informed him that Jesus the Nazarene was passing by. So
he called out to Jesus, the Son of David, to have pity on him. Even
though the people surrounding this beggar scolded him and insisted that he keep quiet, he shouted louder. When Jesus heard him,
Jesus did not assume he knew what this blind man wanted,
although it was obvious to everyone else that the blind man wanted to see. Instead, Jesus bestowed dignity on the man by having
him speak for himself. (All too often, the dominant culture assumes
that it knows what is best for the marginalized; hence it creates
programs and begins projects to help the poor, never stopping to
ask what kind of help those who are marginalized believe they really need!) In this case, the blind man requested his sight. Jesus
responded, "Your faith has saved you."

The salvation of the poor and outcast is tied to their dependence on Christ. The two rich men, who serve as bookends to this central message, were also asked to depend totally on Christ; because they had much, much was expected. It is easier for the poor, who have nothing, to imitate and follow the disenfranchised status of Jesus than for the rich to follow by disengaging from the security—even though it is false—of their wealth. The first man refused, preferring to depend on his own power and privilege, choosing to maintain a facade of religiosity by keeping the commandments. The second rejected his unethically earned status by committing himself to justice. He immediately began to dismantle the structures created to benefit him. Salvation ceases to be knowledge, recognition, or acceptance of God's incarnation in the personhood of Jesus; rather, salvation is linked to what Jesus did for the marginalized of his time and ours. Salvation is grounded in imitating the actions Jesus took toward bringing about liberation, not in the intellectual acceptance of a belief.

OF SHEEP AND GOATS

Matthew 25:31–46 describes the last day when the risen Christ will return to earth in all his splendor, escorted by the host of heaven, to take his seat on the throne of glory. All the nations will be assembled before him as he separates people from one another as a shepherd separates the sheep from goats. The sheep he will place on his right hand, and the goats on his left. Then the ruler of all will say to those on his right hand, "Come, you whom my Father considers blessed, take for your heritage the reign prepared for you since the foundation of the world. For I was hungry and you gave me food; I was thirsty and you gave me drink; I was an alien and you made me welcome; naked and you clothed me, sick and you visited me, in prison and you came to see me."

But to those on his left hand he will say, "Depart from me you cursed ones, to the eternal fire prepared for the devil and his demons. For I was hungry and you never gave me food; I was thirsty and you never gave me anything to drink; I was an alien and you turned me out, naked and you never clothed me, sick and in prison and you never visited me." And when both the virtuous and condemned ask when they did these things to Jesus, Christ will respond, "Truly I say to you, inasmuch as you did it to one of these, the least of my people, you did it to me."

Jesus does not divide sheep from goats by their denominational affiliation, by the church they attended, or by their confession
of faith. The litmus test is what they did or did not do to the least,
to the poorest. Jesus asks if the individual participated in liberative
acts that led others toward an abundant life or if he or she instead
participated in enslaving acts that led others to death. He specifically asks if we fed the hungry, gave water to the thirsty, welcomed
the alien, clothed the naked, visited the sick or the prisoner behind
bars. The radicalness of salvation, as we already saw with the account
of the rich young ruler and Zacchaeus, is that Jesus judges all people on how they interacted with the disenfranchised in society. The
epistle of James best summarizes what awaits those who, like the
rich young ruler, rely on their wealth and religiosity, ignoring the
plight of the marginalized:

> You who are rich, start howling and crying aloud over the
> hardships that are coming to you. Your wealth is rotted, and
> your garments have become moth-eaten. Your gold and sil-
> ver have corroded, and this same corrosion will be your sen-
> tence, eating your flesh as fire. You heaped treasures in the
> last days. Laborers who reaped your fields had their wages
> withheld by you, behold their cries! The cries of those labor-
> ers have entered into the ears of the Lord of hosts. On earth
> you lived luxuriously and lived riotously. In the time of
> slaughter you ate to your heart's content. You condemned,
> you murdered the just, who offered you no resistance.
> (5:1–6)

Our first reaction in reading the above text might be a sigh of
relief. We may say that we are not rich but middle-class, and so this
passage does not apply to us, it applies to those in a higher tax
bracket: the Donald Trumps of the world. I will insist, however,
that it does apply to the vast majority of those living in the so-called
first world, including people on the margins. Specifically, many
people residing in the United States live in a luxury unknown to
the rest of the world and unfathomed by the aristocracy of any previous age. This is made obvious when we consider that the aver-
age yearly income is about $330 in Kenya, $300 in India, or $160
in Bangladesh. In fact, the majority of the world's inhabitants,
about three billion people, live on less than two dollars a day, with

thirty-four thousand children dying each day of hunger and preventable diseases. Living within the United States privileges its inhabitants, making the majority of them the equivalent of the rich young ruler when compared with the rest of the population that shares this planet.

The dichotomy between the privileged few in the industrial nations and the vast majority of the poor throughout the world has led Choan-Seng Song, a theologian from Taiwan, to ask how a church that profits from a rich and affluent society can find solidarity with a God who suffers and dies with the victims of global economic injustices? How can a church in an affluent nation like the United States follow the God of the crucified people? Eurocentric theologies fail to adequately answer, much less wrestle, with these questions.[3] Through metaphoric rather than material readings, these questions are often dismissed. What liberative actions (praxis) are called for so that the rich young rulers of today can inherit eternal life?

Communal Essence of Justice

For people on the margins, seeking justice is an important component in being a Christian. Unfortunately, the concept of justice is sometimes lost when biblical texts are read in English. In English, the Hebrew and Greek terms that denote the concept of justice are usually translated as the ambiguous word "righteous" or "righteousness." Nevertheless, when Latina/os, for example, read biblical texts in Spanish, they discover that the concept of justice is retained in the translation of the word as *justicia*. Consequently, when Euroamericans read "righteous" or "righteousness" in their Bibles, Hispanics read "just" or "justice." Now, the word "righteous" implies an action that can be performed privately. Justice, however, can only be exercised in community, never in isolation. Justice can only manifest itself in relation to others. While a hermit can be righteous by remaining conscientious and God-fearing in thought, a hermit cannot practice justice in isolation because others are needed to whom justice can be administered. Instead of being a private expression of faith, justice becomes a public action, a public manifestation of God's acting grace.

By using the words *justo* and *justicia*, the Spanish translation reinforces communalism as opposed to individualism. For example, the epistle of James tells us that "the prayer of the righteous is powerful and effective" (5:16), that is, the one who is pious has his prayers answered. When we read the same verse in Spanish it is the prayer of the *just one* (the one doing justice within the community in obedience to God) that has much power. In English, Matthew quotes Jesus as saying, "Blessed are those who hunger and thirst for righteousness, for they will be filled" (5:6). In the minds of most in the dominant culture, those who hunger and thirst for moral purity are the ones who will be rewarded. In Spanish, it is those who hunger for justice to be done to all members of the community, especially to the disenfranchised, and who thirst for justice against all oppressors, that God will fully satisfy.

The English text of Luke tells us of the centurion who, witnessing Christ's crucifixion, proclaimed, "Certainly this man was righteous" (23:47). Christ was the unsoiled innocent lamb who died for our sins. In Spanish, this same centurion says, "Certainly this was a just man." Christ was a just man who died an unjust death. The advice given in 1 Timothy in English reads, "The law is laid down not for the righteous but for the lawless and disobedient, for the ungodly and sinful, for the unholy and profane" (1:19). While the English-speaking reader is assured that the law does not apply to her or him because by faith in Christ he or she has been justified and is neither ungodly, sinful, unholy, nor profane, the Spanish reader understands the passage as stating that the individual practicing justice does not need the law, for the law is already internal and her or his actions are only an outward expression of inward conversion.[4]

To read the Bible from the margins becomes an act of faith derived from two sources: a marginalized location (reality) and a paradigm (ideal) derived by the community of faith, a model based on justice. The communal expression of faith avoids the Euroamerican pitfall of a utilitarian individuality that relegates religion to the private sphere, transforming the public Christ into a personal Savior. It is at the cross where reality and idealism intersect. Rather than attempting to define and explain the mystery of Jesus on a cross, those residing in the margins of society attempt to define themselves in light of this mystery. Conversion is not a call to a new religion founded by Jesus; it is a call to a radically subversive lifestyle. Conversion constructs a life existence within a sacred space created both by reality and by the power of the ideal, a space transcending nature, the senses, and our ability to rationalize.

All too often, the social location of the poor, specifically their spirituality, is romanticized. Yet their salvation arises when their quest for liberation from oppressive structures intersects with the action (praxis) of Christ, who willingly hung from a cross. Salvation is found in solidarity with those on the margins who discover a Christ who is also marginalized and crucified. Hence faith becomes a special form of consciousness containing specific consequences for the will. Satisfaction of intellectual needs ceases to be the ultimate goal. Rather, the longing of the heart to answer the unanswerable questions caused by an existence alienated from the earth's resources becomes a religious quest for meaning.

ARE YOU SAVED?

Sin opposes God's benevolent purposes for creation and is responsible for the corruption of God's created order. Sin destroys fellowship with God and with other human beings, and thus it cannot be eradicated except by the unmerited redemptive love of God, received by faith and in communion with one another.[5] Sin as alienation from God is manifested as injustice and oppression toward our fellow human beings. Scholars from the margins usually construct well-defined categories as to who are the perpetrators of injustices and who are the victims. However, there is also a tendency among some theologians on the margins to identify the sins of the dominant Euroamerican culture while overlooking the sins of their own communities, specifically their own brands of sexism, racism, and classism.

Paul reminds us in his letter to the Romans "that all have sinned and come short of the glory of God" (3:23). The plight of those who live on the margins is glamorized when they are seen purely as being noble, devoid of sin. A danger exists of structuring the reality of those who are disenfranchised as only victims. If in fact, because they are marginalized, they then have nothing to confess and do not have a need to seek salvation, then we have romanticized their existence. Yet, even within marginalized groups, internal structures of oppression exist. If we define sin as injustice, caused by broken vertical and horizontal relationships, then we are indeed all sinners. The broken horizontal relationship manifests the original broken vertical relationship with the Creator. Because sin is the source of social injustice and human oppression, it rejects fellowship with God, consequently causing a rejection of fellowship with other humans.[6]

God's reign can be understood as community, people created to live in a positive relation with the divine and with each other. The nemesis of this order is the reduction of individuals to their economic value. This is the basis of sin; hence the writer of 1 Timothy writes, "The root of all evil is the love of money" (6:10). Likewise, Amos observes that the love of money leads the powerful to "trade the poor for a pair of sandals" (2:6). Today person-to-person relationships are often abandoned for subject-to-object relationships. Those who are privileged by society, either consciously or unconsciously, transform everything, including humans, into objects for possession, domination, and domestication. As disposable objects, humans are measured by their production value, with the profit generated going to the one who controls these objects. This "praxis of domination" causes separation from God and separation within the community created by God.[7]

The cross does not exist for the earth's downtrodden to figure out why it is there or why Jesus had to hang from it. Rather, the cross exists to show the marginalized how their sufferings, their rejection by the privileged of society, and their death become the suffering, rejection, and death of God. Those who are disenfranchised can have faith in a God who intimately knows their pain because God experienced their pain, creating a solidarity with those who are oppressed.

Even those who benefit from oppression are welcome to participate in this solidarity! Salvation for the dominant culture is linked to those who are oppressed. The crucified people become Jesus Christ in the here and now. Their suffering has the potential of redeeming the dominant culture by providing it with an opportunity to interact with Christ manifested in the lives and struggle of those living on the margins of society. As those with power die to their privilege and seek solidarity with those who suffer under oppressive structures, they begin to discover Christ.

In a culture that privileges those who are male, those who are wealthy, and those who are white, solidarity with Christ—who forsook his own equality with God to take the form of a human—requires Christ's disciples also to "take up their cross" and follow him. In short, it requires dying to whatever creates privilege and prevents solidarity with the crucified people of today. Salvation, as liberation, requires crucifying maleness, riches, and whiteness—in other words, the active dismantling of any social structure designed to privilege one group at the expense of another. For example, as a male, I recognize that society privileges me solely because I am male. All things being equal, I as male prevail over women in the marketplace and in the church community, whether I like it or not. Being a feminist and reciting pro-women rhetoric is insufficient as long as my *complicity with the status quo* continues to privilege me. Salvation for me, then, becomes linked to ending my old life, a life where I enjoyed the advantages of being male. I die to my maleness—that is, I crucify my old life—*only* by the praxis (actions) I undertake to dismantle the very structures designed to benefit me. Through this process of working to end not only my individual participation in oppression but also my society's participation in oppression, I work out my salvation "in fear and trembling."

But how?

CHAPTER 7

Can't We All Just Get Along?

On March 3, 1991, a bystander videotaped the scene of four white
Los Angeles police officers beating a subdued black man named
Rodney King. Before that night, police brutality, a reality among
people of color, was mostly ignored by the dominant culture, who
refused to believe such things existed. Now the brutality was captured on tape and embedded in the nation's consciousness. To this
day, the beating of Rodney King remains a symbol of police brutality and racial conflict.

A year later, the four officers responsible for the savage beating
of Rodney King were acquitted. The suppressed anger of Los Angeles's disenfranchised community exploded with violence in one of
the worst race riots ever to grip a U.S. city. By May 2, 1992, as the
smoke from thousands of fires lessened, fifty-five people lay dead,
2,382 people were injured, and over $1 billion in property dam-
age had occurred. During the height of the violence, Rodney King
went on television and uttered his now famous plea, "Guys, can't
we all just get along?"

One of the political victims of the 1992 Los Angeles race riots
was the police chief, Daryl Gates, who was eventually forced to
resign. A decade later, reflecting on the events that led to the riots,
Gates defiantly concluded, "[King] got whacked a few extra times
[but he] brought it on himself."[1] How can we get along when
those who are placed in positions of power refuse to acknowledge
that a problem exists? When the fault of police brutality is placed
upon the victim, who brought the "whacking" upon himself? When
no apology is given?

Still, Rodney King's plea for unity continues to haunt us today.
Can't we all just get along? As long as the dominant culture refuses

to accept the reality that it benefits from social structures designed to enhance its power and privilege, then no, we cannot all get along. As long as the nation's sins of racism, classism, and sexism continue to remain masked, then no, we cannot get along. As long as this society avoids reconciliation through dismantling oppressive structures, then no, we cannot get along. We continue to exist as a vastly divided nation that sits on a powder keg ready to explode when the next Rodney King occurs, as most recently happened on the streets of Cincinnati when a nineteen-year-old unarmed black man was shot by the police for a traffic violation. What awaits us if we continue to insist on coexisting as two nations, segregated and unequal? Jesus says it best in Matthew: "Every government divided against itself is brought to ruin, and every city or house divided against itself will not stand" (12:25).

THE DYSFUNCTIONAL FAMILY

A dysfunctional family is usually one being torn apart by a secret everyone knows about but refuses to voice out loud. Dad has a mistress, mom is an alcoholic, sister is a drug addict, or uncle Joe is a child molester. These examples create tension within the family, even as the family pretends nothing is wrong and continues to operate under a facade of normalcy. Without expressing what no one wants to hear yet everyone knows, the family can never begin to work out its problems. Eventually, cracks develop in the family's public persona as it rushes toward disintegration. With time, the family falls apart as each member, wounded by the encounter, attempts to create a new life apart from the family. Wounds that are ignored simply fester, leading individuals toward unhealthy or destructive behavior and lifestyles.

Like a dysfunctional family, this society also has its own dirty little secrets: racism, classism, and sexism. Everyone knows they exist, but seldom do we want to talk about them or take responsibility. What the dominant culture basically wants is for people who have suffered under oppressive structures to simply forgive and forget so that society can move on. But can those who are disenfranchised simply forgive and forget? To do so prevents reconciliation from ever occurring, a reconciliation that is needed if we as a society seek a healthy and abundant life.

FORGIVE AND FORGET?

Many marriages run into trouble because of a lack of communication between the spouses. For example, let us say that the husband does something that either irritates his wife or causes her some type of emotional pain. Typically, the husband may be oblivious to the offense perpetrated, even though his wife's feelings remain hurt. At first, she may keep her silence, hoping her husband would recognize his insensitivity and attempt to rectify his behavior. Unfortunately for her, and for her husband as well, the husband may see no reason to change. After a while, she might gently approach him in an attempt to share her feelings so that he could be more responsive to her needs and concerns. Here is a typical conversation that might take place.

Wife: Honey, remember the other day when you made that comment about me in front of your friends? Well, it hurt me.

Husband: I'm sorry. Let's kiss and make up.

Wife: Sweetheart, I appreciate your apology, but I really don't think you understand how much your comments hurt.

Husband: I do, I do; look, I'm really sorry. Now how about that kiss.

Wife: Precious, I don't think you realize how your comments are a symptom of a recurring theme. It would help me if you heard me explai . . .

Husband: Okay, okay, I said I was sorry; what else do you want?

Wife: I want you to hear me, I want you to . . .

Husband: Look, I apologized already. Can't you be a good Christian and forgive me? Can't we just move on?

Sounds familiar? A similar dialogue occurs between those who live on the margins of society and those who occupy the centers of power and privilege. The disenfranchised are attempting to enter into a dialogue with those who are privileged, hoping to express deep-seated grievances, which the dominant culture usually refuses to acknowledge. The dominant culture (like the husband in the above dialogue) refuses to examine or, at times, even to acknowledge the power it uses to its advantage. This is the power used to direct the discourse, the power to label the other person, the power not to see a need to repent, and the power to become the "real" victim. Rather than deal with these issues of power, the husband in the above dialogue sought forgiveness, which cost him nothing, but his wife everything. The same is true concerning the dominant culture's pursuit of easy forgiveness. And like the wife in the above dialogue, those who exist on the margins of society are the ones who pay the price.

Power to Direct the Discourse

In the above dialogue, the husband simply did not want to recognize his wife's claim that he was responsible for causing her pain. Probably, in his mind's eye, he conceived himself to be a good husband, a sensitive man, a "good catch." How lucky his wife was to be married to an honest, God-fearing man like himself. How ungrateful of her not to appreciate all he has done for her! For her even to suggest that he was the cause of her pain was a shock. It might have even debunked his carefully constructed identity. If she was even remotely right, then he could not be as good as he imagined himself to be. Rather than explore this possibility, he preferred to move on. In like fashion, a good part of the dominant culture honestly believes that it is responsible for providing many good things for those who live on the margins of society. In most cases, the dominant culture does not stop to even consider that it may be causing pain to those who are disenfranchised. Such an assertion questions the moral fabric of many who see themselves as religiously committed. Hence, the haste to move on and just get along.

Those in the center of power and privilege are able to set the terms as to what constitutes the proper topics to be addressed, the type and tone of discussion that are appropriate, the questions and concerns that are to be formulated and raised, what constitutes a proper answer or response, and how the ultimate goal of the discussion (reconciliation) will be achieved. If those who hold grievances are unwilling to abide by how the discourse is constructed, then a conversation will not be possible until they learn how to express themselves properly. How then do those who are on the margins of society find their own voice?

Power to Name

I recall one day when a learned Euroamerican colleague invited me to lunch. Although I was aware that he vehemently disagreed with many of my perspectives on biblical texts, I welcomed the opportunity to discuss those differences. Early in our conversation, on the way to the restaurant, he asked me why I was so angry. What had happened in my life to cause my anger? The question floored me. I always thought of myself as a happy, fun-loving person. Why would he perceive me as angry? For over half of the time we spent together, I tried to prove that I was not angry. It wasn't until afterward that I realized what had occurred. My colleague had wielded the power to name me. By labeling me as angry, my perspective ceased to be valid. Anything I had to say was a product of my so-called anger, as opposed to rigorous scholarship or reflection. As long as the biblical interpretations of people on the margins are reduced to a product of collective anger, then their perspectives can easily be dismissed as unscholarly with little if no relevance to the overall biblical discourse. The power to label becomes the power to control and the power to silence.

Power Not to See a Need to Repent

When the wife in the above dialogue attempted to explain how her husband's actions caused her pain, he really did not want to hear it. He sought forgiveness for whatever she perceived was his transgression. Frankly, he didn't think he had done anything wrong. Like former police chief Darly Gates, he blamed the victim for her misfortune. As mentioned, through the power of labeling, he reduced his wife's concerns, dismissing anything of value that she had to say. Consequently, there was no real need for him to repent. Nevertheless, he probably thought he would apologize so as to appease her and allow them to simply move on. Yet, as the dialogue indicates, his wife refused forgiveness; she sought reconciliation instead, a painful process that can lead to healing.

My unwillingness to forgive the dominant culture for its racial and ethnic abuses is based on the biblical mandate to become one body in Christ, whose prerequisites include salvation (liberation) and reconciliation. Yet the major obstacle to reconciliation is the dominant culture's refusal even to see a need to repent. While people on the margins have always recognized the reality of police brutality—and long before Rodney King's beating was captured on tape—even the videotape proved to be insufficient for bringing about change. Reports continue to tell of an unarmed African in New York being shot over forty times by police, or a Latino man in Philadelphia having his head crushed while in the backseat of a police cruiser, or a Haitian immigrant in New York having a toilet plunger inserted in his rectum while under arrest at the police station, or drug squad officers in Pittsburgh planting evidence on suspects and falsified reports; and the list goes on.

On October 6, 1998, Amnesty International released a 153-page report accusing the United States of systematically violating the human rights of its citizens, specifically its citizens of color. The violations include mistreatment of prisoners, excessive use of police force, detention of asylum seekers, execution of children, and the providing of arms and training to repressive regimes. Amnesty's secretary-general, Pierre Sané, in his report to the United Nations said, "Human rights violations in the United States of America are persistent, widespread, and appear to disproportionately affect people of racial or ethnic minority backgrounds."[2]

In spite of these accusations, the dominant culture is offended that the world community would level such charges against a political system that sees itself as the bedrock of truth, justice, and the "American way." After all, it is the United States, the self-proclaimed lighthouse of liberty to a darkened world, that is the moral conscience of the world, quick to point out the human-rights violations that occur specifically in those nations that are not our allies. Yet, when the earth's marginalized question the integrity of the United States, we are incredulous. We usually respond by withholding payments to the United Nations to teach them not to question our "righteous" motives. Nowhere in the discourse is the option of repenting for the human-rights violations toward people of color even considered.

Power to Become the "Real" Victim

Robert H. Bork, the conservative legal jurist whom then president Ronald Reagan nominated to the U.S. Supreme Court but whose nomination was defeated in Congress, wrote once that the only group that is truly oppressed in the United States today is white, heterosexual males. Providing a voice to many in the dominant culture, Bork accused people on the margins of participating in a rhetoric of victimhood so as to force Euroamericans to seek absolution from those they have supposedly oppressed. He added that such actions by people on the margins lead to the vilification of all Euroamericans. Those college or university professors dealing with issues of race "teach resentment and fear [and their] careers would be diminished or ended by progress in racial reconciliation; [hence it is to these professors' best interest] to preserve and exacerbate racial antagonism."[3]

By recasting themselves as victims, victimizers are free from having to deal with how societal structure privileges them. Bork refuses to recognize that Euroamericans are not the only ones who "belong" in the United States while others simply live here. When those on society's margins attempt to establish a dialogue to investigate how they too can inhabit this country as full and equal citizens, power holders whose power is jeopardized by such assertions begin to cast themselves as the victims, while labeling those seeking dialogue as "race hustlers." They see themselves under the "tyranny" of those who have historically been oppressed but who now, according to Bork, have greater opportunities to advance but instead blame whites for all of their problems.

Euroamericans are, indeed, victims, but not victims in the sense Bork intended. Instead, they are victims of the very structures designed to protect their power and privilege. According to Thandeka, a minister and black theologian, from a young age, children are taught their place in society and how they should relate to others. In most communities the "white" norm is taught as the legitimate way to interact with others. As this norm is taught, children are forced to suppress their natural inclinations to play and relate with each other at daycare or school. In kindergarten, children naturally play together regardless of race or gender, but by the time they reach high school, they have been taught and conditioned to sit at different tables in the school cafeteria. They learn to mistrust their co-students because they fear being exiled from their own community. "You better not date a black man or I'll disown you," the parent may verbally or nonverbally communicate to the child. Or children may learn to remain silent or offer up nervous laughter as the usual response to racist jokes, slurs, or abuse.

Euroamericans, seeing themselves as the norm, are, in effect, raceless; that is, everyone else is "colored," while they have no color. For example, the dominant culture refers to the black cop, the Hispanic teacher, or the Asian mechanic. Seldom does it refer to the white cop, the white teacher, or the white mechanic, mostly because the norm of whiteness makes everyone white unless otherwise stated. Yet, when children reach adulthood, they must begin to deal with the contradictory racial statements, emotions, and mental states that arise from reconciling the need to belong to their group with how they are taught to deal with those of other groups.[4]

The societal structures that cause oppression are not reducible to a formula where only those who are marginalized are the victims. Although it is impossible to equate the suffering of those who are disenfranchised with those who are privileged, it is important to note that those at the center of society are also victims of these structures. They too are indoctrinated to believe they deserve, or earn, or have a right to power and privilege. They are trapped into living up to the false ideal of superiority and so require the same liberation yearned for by the disenfranchised. Even those who are not economically privileged are taught to dream upward, aspiring to become wealthy and to associate with the society's elite, even as they blame downward, accusing those who are marginalized of stealing their jobs and depressing wages, thus preventing them from achieving their rightful place in society. This is a primary reason programs designed to rectify societal structures, like affirmative action, face such vehement resistance.

Cheap Forgiveness

In the above dialogue between husband and wife, the wife attempted to discuss what was bothering her. No doubt, the husband probably did not enjoy such encounters, hearing how he caused her pain. Most who find themselves in similar situations desire to be forgiven so as to avoid the unpleasantry of a matrimonial conflict. Whatever insincere apology that can be mustered is gladly given to pacify her. Regardless of how many apologies offered, the wife in the above dialogue refused to offer a forgiveness that fell short of dealing with the recurring learned behavior that needed alteration. She was determined instead to seek reconciliation so that these problems could indeed be put behind them, allowing them the opportunity to renew their relationship and grow together. Likewise, those who call themselves Christians and desire to become one body in Christ must seek reconciliation rather than cheap forgiveness. At times forgiveness must be withheld before reconciliation can occur.

In Matthew 5:23–24, Jesus instructs the faithful to move beyond religiosity by reconciling with those who hold grievances: "If, then, you offer your gift on the altar, and there remember that your companion has something against you, leave your gift there before the altar, and go. First be reconciled to your companion, and then come offer your gift." The emphasis is not on whether the religious person remembers committing an offense but, rather, on whether the offended party had a complaint against the worshiper. The responsibility is to seek reconciliation before coming to God once one is made aware that an offense exists. Those who read the Bible from the margins have given notice that they are offended by racist, sexist, and classist structures and await the good church-going Christians of the dominant culture to leave their sacrifices at the altar and seek them out to establish reconciliation.

All the dominant culture accomplishes by cheap forgiveness is the creation of a multicultural facade where we occasionally may gather to hold hands and sing "Kumbaya." But it always ends the same, with everyone returning to their segregated lives. Racism, classism, and sexism continue to be society's dirty secret, as injustices continue. We continue to pat ourselves on the back celebrating how much has been accomplished in establishing "justice for all" when all the while we continue to disintegrate as a society.

And what about the church? It abrogates its mandate to become one body in Christ and leads believers further away from the living God. First John reminds us, "Anyone claiming to be in the light, yet hating his fellow human, is still in the darkness" (2:9). To be saved means to be reconciled with the God we cannot see and our fellow human beings whom we can see. A lack of reconciliation is a sign of absent salvation. Because cheap forgiveness never leads to reconciliation, it can never lead to salvation. However, by listening carefully to the voiceless, the dominant culture can learn something about itself that might lead it to a salvific understanding of the biblical message.

WHAT THE CENTER CAN LEARN
ABOUT THE BIBLE

All too often, those who occupy the center of power and privilege find the interpretations generated from the margins of society to be reductionist. These interpretations are at times perceived to be reduced to political positions that are contrary to the interest of the dominant culture. Such critiques ignore that the disenfranchised ascribe to their biblical interpretations an inclusiveness that requires both a spiritual and a political response to injustice. Reading the biblical texts leads believers to judge and condemn any present oppressive structures that cause death to segments of the population. One cannot remain silent while God's people are crucified. Rather, the hope for salvation and liberation forces the Bible reader to claim the recurring themes found throughout the book. The themes that serve as the foundation for how marginalized communities read the text also serve as a corrective to the highly individualistic and spiritual interpretations coming from the center of society. Four related themes about God inform how society is challenged by the way marginalized groups read biblical texts. These texts reveal a God who is the liberator, the seeker of justice, the doer, and the subverter.

Exodus: God the Liberator

The God of Exodus is not some abstract, impassive cosmic Being that utterly transcends the human dilemma. The God of Exodus is a God who actively entered human history to side with the oppressed slaves of Egypt and lead them personally toward the promised land of their liberation. God's movement, which brings about the liberation of the Hebrews, was a political action with political consequences impacting the socioeconomic ethos of Egypt. It was the breaking away from a situation of despoliation and misery and the beginning of the construction of a just and fraternal society. It was the suppression of disorder and the creation of a new order.[5]

Salvation was no longer limited to the soul in a life hereafter; rather, salvation encompassed liberation from the misery caused by the oppressive political structures that privileged the Egyptians. God acted in history to make history, a history that revealed a God who is foremost a liberator of God's people. Prior to giving the Ten Commandments to the emerging nation of Israel at Mt. Sinai, God revealed Godself to the people by saying, "I am Yahweh your God who has brought you out from the land of Egypt, from the house of bondage." The God of the Hebrews introduced Godself as the liberator who freed the oppressed from the house of bondage when God gave the most important portion of Hebrew law.

God took the first step in choosing the lowly Hebrews so as to tie God's will with the liberation of a politically and socially oppressed people. Just as God entrusted the Ten Commandments to this oppressed group so that through them God could be revealed to all of humanity, so too are the marginalized of society chosen to become the instrument by which God the liberator is revealed today. But the message of liberation, as crucial as it is to the very essence of God, is not offered for the sake of liberation alone. Those who are disenfranchised are not just liberated from something; they are liberated for a purpose: to become the means by which the rest of humanity can discover the God who acts within history so that all can be liberated, even the oppressors who benefit from those structures.

Amos: God the Seeker of Justice

One of the salient characteristics about the message of the prophets in the Hebrew Bible is the connection they made between the judgment of God and the nation's neglect of those who are most marginalized, referred to as the orphans, the widows, and the aliens. Isaiah demands that a sinful nation "seek justice, reprove the oppressor, judge the orphan, contend for the widow" (1:17). Jeremiah, answering the question as to why God's punishment is falling upon the House of Jacob, states, "[The elite center] have become great and grown rich. . . . They ignore evil deeds, they do not plead for the cause of the orphan so that they may prosper, nor do they uphold the cause of the poor" (5:27–28). According to Ezekiel, among the crimes of Jerusalem that led to its destruction was that "the people of the land have used oppression and practiced robbery; they have troubled the poor and needy, and have oppressed the alien denying them justice" (22:29). This theme continues through the minor prophets. Although an examination of this theme among the Hebrew prophets is beyond the scope of this book, we can focus on one prophet, Amos, as a representative of the whole.

The Hebrew prophets proclaimed that God identifies with those who suffer under unjust structures. The prophet Amos was not concerned that the religious folks of his time showed charity to those who were marginalized; rather, he called for the creation of a new and just socioeconomic structure:

> Hear this, you who trample the poor and silence the humble of the earth. You who say, "When will the New Moon pass so that we may sell grain, or the Sabbath so we can market our wheat?" By diminished bushel and raised currency, by falsifying and tampering with the scales, you buy the helpless with silver, and the poor for a pair of sandals. Even getting paid for the sweeping of the wheat. Yahweh has sworn by the pride of Jacob, "Never will I forget all these things you have done" (8:4–7).

Those who belonged to the dominant culture of Amos's time were good people who were faithful in their religiosity. They attended worship and offered sacrifices, yet they reconciled religious practices with an economic system that benefited them at the expense of others. For this reason, Amos informs the people that God was not appeased by their rituals; rather, God finds satisfaction only in the establishment of justice.

> I hate, I reject your feast days, and I will not delight in your festive assemblies. Even if you offer up to me burnt offerings or food offerings, I will not be pleased. I will not look upon your peace offerings of fattened animals. Take away from me the sound of your songs, and the melody of your harps, I will not hear them. Instead, let justice roll down like water, and righteousness like an ever-flowing torrent. (5:21–24)

Amos was not popular among the religious people of the dominant culture. Amos was an alien, a Judean from south of the border preaching in the northern nation of Israel. He had no religious training, being neither a prophet nor a prophet's son; instead he worked in the field, a shepherd who tended sycamore trees (7:14–15). Amos, an alien with a menial job, would be the equivalent today of an undocumented Latino, maybe working as a gardener in the exclusive suburbs of Washington, D.C., going to the National Cathedral to deliver God's message of justice.

When the promised land was first settled by the Israelites, the land was distributed equally among the tribes and families so that everyone could have a similar living standard. Nevertheless, by the time of Amos, large luxurious houses were found on one side of town while smaller and poorer houses were clustered together on the other side, similar to what can be found in any major city or community in the United States. A small segment of the population lived in complacency, blind to the marginalization of their compatriots; they enjoyed the security of wealth accumulated through a social structure designed to enrich them at the expense of others.

> Woe to those who are at ease in Zion, and to those who place their trust on the mountains of Samaria; . . . those lying on beds of ivory, and those sprawled on their couches; those eating lambs from the flock and stall-fattened veal. They howl to the harp, they invent new instruments of music like David. They drink bowls of wine, and anoint themselves with the best oils, but they do not grieve over the ruin of Joseph! (6:1, 4–6)

At this point in history, during the reign of Jeroboam II, Israel was at the zenith of its power. It was militarily and economically secure and faced no immediate foreign threat, much like the United States after the Cold War. In the midst of this false security, a voice was raised from the underside of Israel, which thought itself a religious nation and took its economic success as proof of God's blessing, that judgment was about to befall it for refusing to establish justice. For this reason Amos was considered a threat to those in positions of power and, as such, had to be dismissed, a task undertaken by the priest of Bethel, Amaziah.

> Then Amaziah, the priest of Bethel, sent word to Jeroboam, king of Israel, saying, "Amos has conspired against you in

the midst of the house of Israel. The land is unable to endure all his words!" . . . And to Amos Amaziah said, "Go, O seer, flee to your own land Judah, and eat there your bread and do your prophesying. Do no more prophesying at Bethel, for this is the royal city which contains the national sanctuary." (7:10, 12–13)

Amos serves as an exemplar of the mission undertaken by all of the biblical prophets. The message of Amos, along with the rest of the Hebrew prophets, denounces injustice. God reveals concern for those who are marginalized and is angered by the injustices committed against them.

Thus says Yahweh, "For three transgressions of Israel, and for four, I will not withdraw from my decree: they sold for silver the just, and the poor for a pair of sandals. They trample upon the dust of the earth and the heads of the helpless, and divert the path of the humble." (2:6–7)

Consequently, God not only calls for justice but stands against the oppressors, even if they are Jews and members of the chosen people. For those who refuse to establish justice, God swears an oath not to side with them.

Hear this word, you cows of Bashan, who from the mountain of Samaria oppress the helpless, crush the poor, and say to their husbands, "Bring us drink." The Lord Yahweh has sworn my God's holiness that the days are coming upon you when God will lift you up with meat hooks, and the very last of you with prongs. (4:1–2)

The justice that Amos demands is usually skewed by social structures designed to protect the wealthy. This message, rooted in the historical customs and traditions of the people, is pregnant with promise of reform for their present oppressive situation. God calls for liberation and salvation at every level of human existence. No one can claim to be a follower, believer, or worshiper of God unless they too seek justice.

> Trouble awaits those who turn justice into wormwood, and abandon the just. . . . They hate the one dispensing justice at the city gate, and reprove the one who speaks up-rightly. Therefore, because you trample the poor, and steal from them their tribute of grain, the houses hewn of stones which you built you shall not dwell in, and the vineyards of desire you have planted, you shall not drink their wine. For I know your many transgressions and your numerous sins of oppressing the righteous, of taking a bribe, and of turning away the poor seeking justice at the city gates. (5:7, 10–12)

Accordingly, the message is powerfully oriented toward the future, toward a completely new encounter with the God of history, an encounter that empowers those who are disenfranchised while bringing the possibility for salvation to those who benefit from oppression.

> Seek good and not evil, so that you may live and that Yahweh, the Lord of hosts, may really be with you as you have claimed. Hate evil and love good and establish justice at the city gates. Perhaps Yahweh the Lord of hosts will be gracious to the remnant of Joseph. (5:14–15)

In the very act of unmasking the not-so-well-hidden oppressive social structures, a new movement toward salvation is initiated for those who benefit from the very structures of oppression. God siding with the oppressed means judgment for the oppressors. Even so, judgment is always accompanied by hope.

> In that day, I will raise up the booth of David that has fallen and wall up its breaches. And its ruin will I raise and I will rebuild it as in the days of old. (9:11)

The Gospels: God the Doer

The Gospel of John begins with a radical proclamation about the very essence of Christ. The first verse clearly states, "In the beginning was the Word, and the Word was with God, and the Word was God" (John 1:1). In English, the Greek term *logos* is usually translated as "word," used in the biblical texts as a noun. Yet *logos* has a wide range of meanings that goes beyond this simple translation. This *logos* became flesh and dwelled among the people (1:14). For the writer of the Gospel of John, the action of creation is assigned to *logos:* "All things through him came into being, and without him, not even one thing came into being" (1:3).

It is interesting to note that if we read the first verse of the Gospel in Spanish, it goes, "*En el principio era el Verbo, y el Verbo estaba con Dios, y el Verbo era Dios*" ("In the beginning was the Verb, and the Verb was with God, and the Verb was God"). Although the English version of the Scriptures exclaims that Jesus is the Word, those who read the Bible in Spanish discover that Jesus is the Verb, nuancing its creative aspect. Feminist theologian Mary Daly asks why we must reduce God to a noun and, by so doing, destroy the dynamic nature of the Verb.[6] Continuing on this theme, Latino theologian Luis Pedraja concludes that if the Deity can indeed be perceived as a Verb, then theology must reflect this active nature.[7]

As the Verb, Jesus becomes the incarnation of God's living and active Verb. Rather than portraying a static noun, an action word is used to remind the reader of the importance of faith as action, as praxis. This has a profound effect on how theology is conceived by Euroamericans and those who read the text in Spanish, specifically Hispanics. For Latina/os, theology can no longer be reduced to abstract concepts about God from which doctrines are derived. Instead, theology becomes something that is done, not believed.[8]

The very biblical text ceases to be a thing (book) and becomes an action, a testimony of God's call to action. When we read the Bible, we do not read a book; rather we are confronted with the action of either obedience or disobedience to Jesus Christ as presented to us through the Gospels. The Bible calls us to liberative actions, actions that seek the abundant life for all of God's creation. Doctrinal interpretations, the product of a metaphoric reading that attempts to reconcile the dominant culture's lifestyle with the biblical message, are debunked by the action of the resurrection, the ultimate manifestation of the new liberative abundant life we are called to, a life determined through a materialist reading of the text.

Acts and the Letters from Paul: God the Subverter

Paul's ministry in Philippi, found in Acts 16:6–15, provides an excellent example of God as the subverter of any religiosity that fails to consider seriously racism, classism, and sexism. According to the Scriptures, Paul set out to evangelize the known world, but the Spirit of God delayed him while at the border of Mysia. There he had a vision. A Macedonian man appeared, beseeching him, "Come across to Macedonia to help us." Paul lost no time and crossed into Macedonia, taking the vision to be God's call.

When Paul reached Philippi, he went to the customary place for Jewish prayer. According to the writer of Acts, Paul went beyond the old city walls to the *proseuchē*, a term used to describe the service of traditional Jewish prayers held during the Sabbath. Such prayers require a minimum number of men to be present. In a sermon, Doctor Loida Martell-Otero, a Baptist minister in the Bronx, revealed the continuous conversion of Paul in this story. A Macedonian *man* told him to cross over and help them. Paul then sought a group of *men* to begin his ministry, but instead he found a bunch of women! Paul was faced with a dilemma. Torah, God's word, was not for women, according to tradition. Yet this was the man who would eventually say that in Christ there is neither male nor female (Gal. 3:28). Paul was forced to give up his traditions and concepts of the divine in order to begin God's ministry. He spoke to the women, and one of them, Lydia, an entrepreneur who had achieved financial success in the production of purple fabric, was converted. And what did she do upon being baptized? She challenged Paul, stating, "If you really think me a true believer in the Lord, come and stay with us." Upon this woman, the church of Philippi was established. In Dr. Martell-Otero words, "The church is being made to convert, even as it seeks converts."[9]

All too often those at the centers of power and privilege look to the margins of society, asking people there to change, to conform, and to assimilate to the way the dominant culture does religion. If the truth resides only in the center, then the margins are the ones that must be converted in order to obtain truth and enter into fellowship with God and God's people. The account in Acts subverted the self-imposed religious superiority of the early church.

As the first Christian church encountered the rest of the world, it was forced to change, to become multicultural so that others could come into a salvific relationship with the God of the universe, not just with the culture of that first church.

This story in Acts raises another question. Can a woman establish and lead a church? Years later Paul wrote a letter to the Philippians. In it he attempted to prevent a schism by appealing to two of the church leaders, Euodia and Syntyche, to reconcile their differences. Then he praised these women for being co-laborers with him in defending the work of the Christ (4:2–3). It appears that not only did a woman start the church at Philippi but that years later women still held leadership positions.

Yet, before we celebrate Paul's "feminism," we must remember that this is the same man who required women to remain silent during church services. Two passages have traditionally been used to prevent women from participating in leadership positions. They are 1 Corinthians, "Let the women in the churches be silent, for it is not allowed for them to speak, but let them be subjected as also the Law says. But if they desire to learn anything, let them question their own husbands at home, for it is a shame for women to speak in church" (14:34–35). And 1 Timothy, "Let a woman learn in silence, in all subjection. But I do not allow her to teach, nor to exercise authority over a man, but rather to be in silence" (2:11–14). Yet Paul subverted his own words by his recognition of the roles women held and by the guidelines he established for women leaders.

While the passages from 1 Corinthians and 1 Timothy are constantly used to continue the silencing of women within the Christian church, numerous other passages that recognize women's leadership are ignored. The question is not whether women can serve as leaders but how Paul can make these statements when he praises so many women leaders. Paul was familiar with the sign of the new church proclaimed by Peter in Acts, "'In the last days,' says God, 'I will pour from my Spirit on all flesh, and your sons *and daughters* will prophesy'" (2:17). The Greek word translated into "prophesy" can better be understood as "preach," when interpreted in its strictest biblical sense. The word "prophesy" is less concerned with predicting some future events than with proclaiming God's words to God's people so that the body of believers know what is required of them.

The pouring out of God's Spirit is marked by both men and women preaching God's word, an action that is prohibited due to sexism in many churches that claim to be filled with the Spirit of God. Yet, during Paul's time, leaders of the church consisted of those who preached the Good News, as in the case of prophets (preachers) and teachers who acted as local leaders, those who managed and ran a church from their home, as in the case of overseers (pastors), and those who traveled from city to city evangelizing, as in the case of apostles (the English transliteration from the Greek means "one who is sent out"). Women throughout the book of Acts and Paul's letters occupied all of these positions, subverting the patriarchal interpretations usually given to the passages, found in 1 Corinthians and 1 Timothy, that called for the silent submission of women.

Paul knew of women who served as church starters, as in the case of Lydia of Philippi (Acts 16:11–12); as teachers, as in the case of Priscilla, one of Apollos' instructors (Acts 18:24–28); as preachers, as in the case of the four daughters of Philip (Acts 21:8–9); and as church elders *(presbyteros),*[10] as in the case of the elected lady (2 John 1–5). Additionally, Paul sent his greetings and encouragements to women who served as deacons, as in the case of Phoebe (Rom. 16:1);[11] as apostles, as in the case of Junia (Rom. 16:7);[12] and as pastors, as in the case of Phoebe the deacon in Cenchreae (Rom. 16:1), Priscilla (along with her husband Aquila) in either Ephesus or Rome (Rom. 16:3–5), Chloe in either Corinth or Ephesus (1 Cor. 1:11), Nympha in Laodicea (Col. 4:15), and Apphia (along with two others) in Colossae (Philem. 1–2).[13] The role these women played would eventually lead to other women serving in the priesthood during the church's first thousand years of history: serving as elders, as in the case of Paniskianes; serving as bishops, as in the case of Bishop Theodora; and serving as patrons underwriting ministerial activities. Some scholars even insist that Priscilla wrote the epistle to the Hebrews. By the third and fourth centuries of the Christian church, the opponents of women clergy succeeded in imposing the prevalent sexism of the secular culture upon the church's structures, thus bringing to an end the mark of the pouring out of the Spirit, the preaching of their "sons and daughters."[14]

Why then does Paul make such misogynic statements in both 1 Corinthians and 1 Timothy? A few chapters prior to Paul's pronouncement in 1 Corinthians 14:34–35 (requiring women to remain silent), he provides guidelines for women who preach before congregations (11:5). Is there a contradiction then in the biblical text? Many biblical scholars have attempted to dismiss the two troublesome passages in 1 Corinthians 14 and 1 Timothy 2 by claiming they were later added to the text. Others simply dismiss Paul. Still others attempt to reconcile any apparent contradictions between these two passages and the numerous references where women, through deed and speech, led the church. Perhaps the two passages were not written to highlight injustices in need of correction or to instruct on what should (or should not) be done within ecclesiastical structures. Instead, perhaps they simply illustrate the consequences of being a woman within a patriarchal society. The struggle by women like Mary Magdalene, Lydia, Priscilla, Phoebe, and Junia to claim their liberation and salvation in Christ from all forms of oppression subverted Paul's words in these two passages. Their actions (praxis) hold the text accountable to the liberating message of Christ's salvation. It could be said that these texts subvert their own forms of oppression.

THE BIBLE IN THE TWENTY-FIRST CENTURY

At an academic conference on the importance of the biblical text to the Latina/o community, one of the participants asked how we scholars could continue to use an ancient text that justifies the oppression of many members of our community, specifically the female members. This question cannot be easily dismissed. The Bible has been used to justify racism, classism, and sexism. Is the Bible beyond redemption? Has its misuse made the text impotent for the twenty-first century? Some liberal scholars would say that the Bible should be rejected because it is an ancient text containing stories, myths, and superstitious pronouncements that simply do not apply in a modern (or postmodern) world. On the other end of the extreme are conservative scholars who ascribe a fundamental literalism to the Bible, maintaining that every word comes directly from the mouth of God. Any apparent contradictions found within the text are a result of human failings or shortcomings, and to question or contradict the text borders on blasphemy.

To read the Bible from the margins is to repudiate both

extremes. Throughout this book, we have challenged the predominant assumption that all biblical interpretations occur apart from, and independent of, the interpreter's social location or identity. Some biblical scholars acknowledge that an interpreter's identity or social location may influence the meaning of the biblical text. For other scholars, a person's identity interferes with the job of ascertaining the hidden yet retrievable message of God. Here the challenge is to put aside the traditional interpretations of the dominant culture and to read the Bible from the margins of society, a reading that counters the claim that the only true meaning of a text can be uncovered apart from what the interpreter brings to the analysis. Some scholars would maintain that such readings from the margins, often based on personal experiences, are unscholarly, yet those who are disenfranchised consistently employ such a strategy *because* it allows their marginalized voices to take center stage. Today it should be recognized that little difference really exists between the private and public voice of the biblical interpreter because all interpretations are either directly or indirectly influenced by one's identity and social location.

How, then, should the marginalized approach biblical texts so that they can be relevant to their lives? In Matthew 9:17 Jesus observes that people do not pour new wine into old wineskins. If they do, the skins will burst, the wine will run out, and the wineskins will be ruined. Instead, new wine is poured into new wineskins so that both can be preserved. Likewise, neither the literalism of a fundamentalist nor the liberal's rejection of the biblical texts as ancient and thus irrelevant serves marginalized societies. These are old wineskins that cannot contain the relatively new way the biblical message is being understood among groups suffering under oppressive social structures.

Today the Bible is increasingly recognized as a complicated text in which many meanings and interpretations struggle with one another, creating tension in how the Bible is to be read and understood. No longer is there general satisfaction with one interpretation held to be universally true for all people in all times. To read the Bible from the margins of society counters the dominant culture's interpretation, which claims its immediate access to the Deity. The interpretations developed from the underside remind the dominant culture that the margins do exist in spite of attempts to exclude them from the discourse. Such a reading seeks neither the permission nor approval of the dominant culture. Rather it is a methodology by which the Bible becomes relevant to those in today's society whose theological perspectives have historically been ignored or dismissed. To ignore this reading condemns us all to the festering consequences of our own racism, classism, and sexism. Reading the Bible from the margins provides a salvific message of liberation for all of humanity by providing the key to combat the oppression of humans by other humans so that all can enjoy the abundant life.

Notes

Introduction

1. The reader should be aware that all scriptural quotes are the translation of the author.
2. Gustavo Gutiérrez, *The Power of the Poor in History,* trans. Robert R. Barr (Maryknoll: Orbis Books, 1984), xi. For Gutiérrez, reading the text from the perspective of those residing in the underside of history reveals two implicit themes. The first is the universality of God's love. The second is God's preferential option for the poor.
3. Justo L. González, *Santa Biblia: The Bible through Hispanic Eyes* (Nashville: Abingdon Press, 1996), 59–60.
4. Miguel A. De La Torre and Edwin D. Aponte, *Introducing Latino/a Theologies* (Maryknoll: Orbis Books, 2001), 19.
5. MTV, *The Real World: New Orleans,* Episode 9.
6. Martin Luther King, Jr., "Letter from Birmingham Jail," in *Why We Can't Wait* (New York: Penguin Books, 1964), 81.

1. Learning to Read

1. Max Weber, *The Sociology of Religion* (Boston: Beacon Press, 1963), 107.
2. Associated Press, "Play Gets Threats for Having Black Jesus," *The Philadelphia Inquirer* (March 5, 1997), R-4.
3. Several books develop this theme of the African presence in the biblical text. See Charles Copher, "The Black Presence on the Old Testament," in *Stony the Road We Trod: African American Biblical Interpretation,* ed. Cain Hope Felder (Minneapolis: Fortress Press, 1991). Also see Shawn Kelly, "Race," in *Handbook of Postmodern Biblical Interpretation,* ed. A. K. M. Adam (St. Louis: Chalice Press, 2000).
4. Sexism refers to social structures and systems where the "actions, practices, and use of laws, rules and customs limit certain activities of one sex, but do not limit those same activities of other people of the other sex." See Sara Shute, "Sexist Language and Sexism," in *Sexist Language:*

A Modern Philosophical Analysis, ed. Mary Vetterling-Braggin (Boston: Littlefield, Adams, and Company, 1981), 27.

5. Scott R. Vrana and David Rollock, "Physiological Response to a Minimal Social Encounter: Effects of Gender, Ethnicity, and Social Context," *Psychophysiology* 35 (1998): 462–469.

6. Luis G. Pedraja, *Jesus Is My Uncle: Christology from a Hispanic Perspective* (Nashville: Abington Press, 1999), 47–48.

7. A similar term exists among other Asian groups. For example, among the Chinese it is known as *hen* and connotes a more extreme passion for vengeance. Among Japanese, *kon* connotes grudge bearing and visible resentment. Vietnamese use the term *han,* defining it like the Koreans.

8. For a complete discussion of *han,* see Andrew Sung Park, *Racial Conflict and Healing: An Asian-American Theological Perspective* (Maryknoll: Orbis Books, 1998).

9. W. E. B. Du Bois, *The Souls of Black Folk* (Grand Rapids: Candace Press, 1996), 7.

10. Michelle Fine and Cheryl Bowers, "Racial Self-Identification: The Effects of Social History and Gender," *Journal of Applied Social Psychology* 14 (2) (March–June 1984): 136–146.

11. Leticia A. Guardiola-Sáenz, "Borderless Women and Borderless Texts: A Cultural Reading of Matthew 15:21–28," *Semeia* 78 (1997): 69–81.

2. Reading the Bible from the Center

1. Although the biblical text does not tell us the type of fruit borne by the tree of the knowledge of good and evil, Eurocentric artists have imagined it to be an apple. I, however, a son of the Caribbean, imagine Eden to be the perfection of the tropical island that witnessed my birth; hence, when I read the creation story through my own eyes, I envision the fruit to be a mango!

2. Ronald J. Sider, *Rich Christians in an Age of Hunger: Moving from Affluence to Generosity* (Nashville: Word Publishing, 1997), 1, 9, 29, 89.

3. "Survey Finds Lingering Racial Inequalities," *The New York Times* (October 3, 1999), A25.

4. Paul Shepard, "Rights Group's Study Links Justice and Race; Want Lawmakers to Act," *The Grand Rapids Press* (May 7, 2000), A5.

5. "Survey Finds Lingering Racial Inequalities," A25.

6. A full discussion of those who are oppressed adopting the image of the dominant culture and emulating them to become the new oppressors can be found in Paulo Freire, *Pedagogy of the Oppressed,* rev. ed., trans. Myra Bergman Ramos (New York: Continuum, 1994), 27–44.

7. Elizabeth Conde-Frazier, "Hispanic Protestant Spirituality," in

Teología en Conjunto: A Collaborative Hispanic Protestant Theology, ed. José David Rodríguez and Loida I. Martell-Otero (Louisville: Westminster John Knox Press, 1997), 139–140.

3. Unmasking the Biblical Justification of Racism and Classism

1. Justo L. González, *For the Healing of the Nations: A Book of Revelation in an Age of Cultural Conflict* (Maryknoll: Orbis Books, 1999), 86–91.

2. During the Age of Exploration, when Europeans explored and conquered the Americas, Africa, and Asia, the popular idea existed that the "savages" these colonizers encountered were soulless humans descended from another "Adam." As "savage," they were economically beneficial to the Europeans because they could neither belong to the family of man nor claim to possess property rights. See Olive Patricia Dickason, "The Concept of *l'Homme Sauvage,*" in *Manlike Monsters on Trial: Early Records and Modern Evidence,* ed. Marjorie M. Halpin and Michael M. Ames (Vancouver: University of British Columbia Press, 1980).

3. Albert J. Raboteau, *Slave Religion: The "Invisible Institution" in the Antebellum South* (Oxford: Oxford University Press, 1978), 96–103.

4. Katie Geneva Cannon, *Katie's Canon: Womanists and the Soul of the Black Community* (New York: Continuum, 1995), 27–46; and Renita J. Weems, "Reading *Her Way* through the Struggle: African American Women and the Bible," in *Stony the Road We Trod: African American Biblical Interpretation,* ed. Cain Hope Felder (Minneapolis: Fortress Press, 1991), 57–77.

5. Many biblical scholars maintain that the Canaanites were not systematically annihilated. Some insist that wandering Hebrews began to migrate into these areas and slowly took over the political structures. Others believe that the former Egyptian slaves were not the only Hebrews and that other groups of Hebrews entered these lands at different times prior to and after the Egyptian Hebrews. Still other scholars believe that the marginalized Canaanites, together with the former Egyptian slaves, rebelled against the political structures of the land. Regardless of what actually happened, the biblical narrative of holy war that sanctioned genocide remains.

6. A bull is defined as an apostolic letter with a leaden seal, written with the authority of the Pope as Christ's representative on earth.

7. Robert Allen Warrior, "A Native American Perspective: Canaanites, Cowboys, and Indians," in *Voices from the Margins: Interpreting the Bible in the Third World,* rev. ed., ed. R. S. Sugirtharajah (Maryknoll: Orbis Books, 1997), 277–285.

8. William Baldridge, "Native American Theology: A Biblical Basis," *Christianity and Culture* (May 28, 1990): 17–18.

9. Kwok Pui Lan, "Discovering the Bible in the Nonbiblical World," in *The Bible and Liberation: Political and Social Hermeneutics,* rev. ed., ed. Norman K. Gottwald and Richard A. Horsley (Maryknoll: Orbis Books, 1993), 17–30. Choan-Seng Song, *Tell Us Our Names: Story Theology from an Asian Perspective* (Maryknoll: Orbis Books, 1987); *Third-Eye Theology: Theology in Formation in Asian Settings,* rev. ed. (Maryknoll: Orbis Books, 1991).

10. Khiok-Khng Yeo, "The Rhetorical Hermeneutic of 1 Corinthians 8 and Chinese Ancestor Worship," in *Voices from the Margins: Interpreting the Bible in the Third World,* ed. R. S. Sugirtharajah (Maryknoll: Orbis Books, 1995), 349–367.

11. Thorstein Veblen, *The Theory of the Leisure Class* (New York: New American Library, 1953), 21–80.

12. Max Weber, *The Protestant Ethic and the Spirit of Capitalism,* trans. Talcott Parsons (New York: Charles Scribner's Sons, 1958), 98–139, 157–163, 175.

13. José Miguez-Bonino, "Marxist Critical Tools: Are They Helpful in Breaking the Stranglehold of Idealist Hermeneutics?" in *Voices from the Margins: Interpreting the Bible in the Third World,* ed. R. S. Sugirtharajah (Maryknoll: Orbis Books, 1995), 60–61.

14. Herbert J. Gans, "The Uses of Poverty: The Poor Pay All," in *Down to Earth Sociology,* 3d ed., ed. James M. Henslin (New York: Free Press, 1991), 336–342.

15. Ronald J. Sider, *Rich Christians in an Age of Hunger: Moving from Affluence to Generosity,* 20th anniv. ed. (Nashville: Word Publishing, 1997), 2, 10, 29, 233.

4. Unmasking the Biblical Justification of Sexism

1. It is not within the scope of this book to reconcile what many Christians notice as being two separate accounts of creation. The first creation story (1:1–2:4) lists the order of creation as follows: day 0—formless void; day 1—light; day 2—the heavens; day 3—land and vegetation; day 4—the sun and moon; day 5—the living creatures in the water and air; day 6—the living creatures on the land and humans (both male and female); day 7—God rested. By contrast, the second creation story (2:5–25) lists the order as day 1—there is land; day 2—water surfaces onto the land; day 3—man; day 4—Eden (plants); day 5—animals; day 6—woman.

2. Although it is important to note that some feminist biblical scholars maintain that "the" *adam,* the first creation, was neither male nor female but both, separated in Genesis 2:21–22 when God creates Eve. See Phyllis Trible, *God and the Rhetoric of Sexuality* (Philadelphia: Fortress Press, 1978), 73.

3. Phyllis Trible, *Texts of Terror: Literary-Feminist Readings of Biblical Narratives* (Philadelphia: Fortress Press, 1984), 65–87.

4. Elsa Tamez, "The Woman Who Complicated the History of Salvation," in *New Eyes for Reading: Reading and Theological Reflections by Women from the Third World,* ed. John S. Pobee and Bärbel Von Wartenberg-Potter (Oak Park, IL: Meyer-Stone Books, 1986), 5–17; Renita J. Weems, *Just a Sister Away: A Womanist Vision of Women's Relationship in the Bible* (San Diego: LuraMedia, 1988), 1–19; and Delores S. Williams, *Sisters in the Wilderness: The Challenge of Womanist God-Talk* (Maryknoll: Orbis Books, 1993).

5. Lewis John Eron, "Homosexuality and Judaism," in *Homosexuality and World Religions,* ed. Arlene Swidler (Valley Forge: Trinity Press International, 1993), 108–114.

6. Denise Carmody and John Carmody, "Homosexuality and Roman Catholicism," in Swidler, *Homosexuality and World Religions,* 137.

7. Elisabeth Schüssler Fiorenza, "1 Corinthians," in *Harper's Bible Commentary,* ed. James L. Mays (San Francisco: Harper & Row, 1988), 1175.

8. Michael S. Piazza, "Nehemiah as a Queer Model for Servant Leadership," in *Take Back the Word: A Queer Reading of the Bible,* ed. Robert E. Goss and Mona West (Cleveland: Pilgrim Press, 2000), 118. Also see John J. McNeill, *The Church and the Homosexual* (Boston: Beacon Press, 1993), 65; and Nancy L. Wilson, *Our Tribe: Queer Folks, God, Jesus, and the Bible* (San Francisco: HarperSanFrancisco, 1995), 124–129.

9. Juan Luis Segundo, *The Liberation of Theology,* trans. John Drury (Maryknoll: Orbis Books, 1976), 8.

5. Who Do You Say I Am?

1. Kathleen Parker, "Jesus Falls Victim to Makeover Madness," *The Grand Rapids Press* (April 14, 2001), A9.

2. James H. Cone, *A Black Theology of Liberation,* 20th Anniversary Edition (Maryknoll: Orbis Books, 1999), 7–10.

3. Cecil Cone, *The Identity Crisis in Black Theology* (Nashville: AMEC, 1975), 37.

4. Ramsay MacMullen, *Roman Social Relations: 50 B.C. to A.D. 284* (New Haven: Yale University Press, 1974), 1–3.

5. Justo L. González, *Santa Biblia: The Bible through Hispanic Eyes* (Nashville: Abingdon Press, 1996), 80–81.

6. Virgilio Elizondo, *Galilean Journey: The Mexican-American Promise,* rev. ed. (Maryknoll: Orbis Books, 2000), 7–18.

7. Origen, *Contra Celsum,* trans. Henry Chadwick (London: Cambridge University Press, 1953), 31–32.

8. Gustavo Gutiérrez, *Las Casas: In Search of the Poor of Jesus Christ*, trans. Robert R. Barr (Maryknoll: Orbis Books, 1993), 62, 96.

9. Achiel Peelman, *Christ Is a Native American* (Maryknoll: Orbis Books, 1995), 13.

10. Ibid., 107–108.

11. George E. Tinker, *Missionary Conquest: The Gospel and Native American Cultural Genocide* (Minneapolis: Fortress Press, 1993), viii.

12. Ibid., 6.

13. Peelman, *Christ Is a Native American*, 102–106.

14. R. S. Sugirtharajah, *Asian Biblical Hermeneutics and Postcolonialism: Contesting the Interpretations* (Maryknoll: Orbis Books, 1998), 22–23.

15. Michael Amaladoss, *Life in Freedom: Liberation Theologies from Asia* (Maryknoll: Orbis Books, 1997), 3–11.

16. Kelly Brown Douglas, *The Black Christ* (Maryknoll: Orbis Books, 1994), 55–64.

17. Thomas Hoyt, "Interpreting Biblical Scholarship for the Black Church Tradition," in *Stony the Road We Trod: African American Biblical Interpretation*, ed. Cain Hope Felder (Minneapolis: Fortress Press, 1991), 29.

18. See Elisabeth Schüssler Fiorenza, "Mary Magdalene: Apostle to the Apostles," *UTS Journal* (April 1975): 22.

19. Elisabeth Schüssler Fiorenza, *But She Said: Feminist Practices of Biblical Interpretation* (Boston: Beacon Press, 1992), 64–65.

20. Mary Daly, *Beyond God the Father: Toward a Philosophy of Women's Liberation* (Boston: Beacon Press, 1973), 69–81.

21. Rosemary Ruether, *Sexism and God-Talk: Toward a Feminist Theology* (Boston: Beacon Press, 1983), 134–138.

22. Elizabeth A. Johnson, *She Who Is: The Mystery of God in Feminist Theological Discourse* (New York: Crossroad, 1998), 72–74, 151.

23. Other references in the Bible where God is described in the feminine are (to name a few) Job 38:29; Isa. 46:3–4; 49:15; 66:13; Hos. 11:3–4; 13:8.

24. John Paul I, *Osservatore Romano* (September 21, 1978), 2.

25. Jacquelyn Grant, "Womanist Jesus and the Mutual Struggle for Liberation," in *The Recovery of the Black Presence: An Interdisciplinary Exploration*, ed. Randall C. Bailey and Jacquelyn Grant (Nashville: Abingdon Press, 1995), 129–142.

26. Chung Hyun Kyung, *Struggle to Be the Sun Again: Introducing Asian Women's Theology* (Maryknoll: Orbis Books, 1991), 64–66.

27. Tom Kenworthy, "Anti-gay Forces Incite Shouting Match at Wyoming Funeral," *The Washington Post* (October 17, 1998), A-3; Mike Soraghan, "Activists, Anti-gay Protestors Exchange Views outside Church," *The Denver Post* (October 17, 1998), A-16; Associated Press,

"Prayers, Protests at Shepard's Funeral," *New York Newsday* (October 17, 1998), A-6; "Anti-gay Protesters Picket Funeral of Beating Victim," *The Ottawa Citizen* (October 17, 1998), A-17.

28. Warren Johansson, "Whoever Shall Say to His Brother Racha (Matthew 5:22)," *Cabirion and Gay Bulletin* 10 (1984): 2–4.

29. In Numbers 21:4–9 the Israelites are punished by fiery serpents whose bites cause death to many. Moses intercedes and, following God's instructions, fashions a bronze serpent and places it upon a standard so that whoever is bitten can gaze upon it and not perish. However, by the reign of Hezekiah, over a half millennium later, this bronze serpent had to be smashed because the Israelites were offering sacrifices to it and calling it Nehushtan (2 Kings 18:4).

6. Jesus Saves

1. Robert N. Bellah et al., *Habits of the Heart: Individualism and Commitment in American Life* (New York: Harper & Row, 1985), 220–221, 334.

2. Billy Graham, *How to Be Born Again* (Waco: Word Books, 1979), 202. (Italics are my own.)

3. Choan-Seng Song, *Third-Eye Theology: Theology in Formation in Asian Settings,* rev. ed., (Maryknoll: Orbis Books, 1990), 182–184.

4. Miguel A. De La Torre and Edwin D. Aponte, *Introducing Latino/a Theologies* (Maryknoll: Orbis Books, 2001), 67–68.

5. Gustavo Gutiérrez, *A Theology of Liberation: History, Politics, and Salvation,* rev. ed., trans. Sister Caridad Inda and John Eagleson (Maryknoll: Orbis Books, 1993), xxxviii.

6. Gustavo Gutiérrez, *We Drink from Our Own Wells: The Spiritual Journey of a People,* trans. Matthew J. O'Connell (Maryknoll: Orbis Books, 1992), 97–102.

7. Enrique Dussel, *Ethics and Community,* trans. Robert R. Barr (Maryknoll: Orbis Books, 1988), 17–19.

7. Can't We All Just Get Along?

1. Daniel Cooney, "Beating Victim Rodney King Reluctant Symbol 10 Years Later," *The Toronto Star* (March 3, 2001).

2. "U.S. Cited for 'Persistent' Rights Abuses," *The Ottawa Citizen* (March 23, 1999), A-9.

3. Robert H. Bork, *Slouching towards Gomorrah: Modern Liberalism and the American Decline* (New York: Regan Books, 1996), 228–229.

4. Thandeka, *Learning to Be White: Money, Race, and God in America* (New York: Continuum, 1999), 11–13.

5. Gustavo Gutiérrez, *A Theology of Liberation: History, Politics, and Salvation*, rev. ed., trans. Sister Caridad Inda and John Eagleson (Maryknoll: Orbis Books, 1993), 155.

6. Mary Daly, "God Is a Verb," *Ms.* 3 (December 1974), 97.

7. Luis G. Pedraja, *Jesus Is My Uncle: Christology from a Hispanic Perspective* (Nashville: Abingdon Press, 1999), 86.

8. Miguel A. De La Torre and Edwin Aponte, *Introducing Latino/a Theologies* (Maryknoll: Orbis Books, 2001), 77.

9. Justo L. González, *Santa Biblia: The Bible through Hispanic Eyes* (Nashville: Abingdon Press, 1996), 51.

10. The Greek word *presbyteros*, translated as "elder," refers to an older church member who has earned the respect of the congregation. As the office of bishop emerged, the elder became an ecclesiastical leader under the bishop's guidance, although Titus 1:5–9 does equate the term "bishop" with "elder." For Catholic historians, *presbyteros* was translated as "priest," while Protestants retain the term "elder" or "presbyter."

11. The fact that Paul begins his greeting of twenty-seven people by first mentioning Phoebe attests to her importance and prominence within Christian circles. The word used to describe Phoebe is *diakonos*, usually translated as "deacon" or "minister" when referring to a male, as in the case of Stephen and the other six men chosen to be deacons by the early church. However, when this same word is used to refer to a woman, for some reason the translators choose to use the word "server." Why? Could the translators of the text be imposing their own sexism in their translation?

12. A literal translation of this verse is as follows: "Greet Andronicus and Junia . . . who are prominent among the apostles." Does this verse mean that Junia is well known by the apostles, or that she is a well-known apostle? The fourth-century bishop of Constantinople John Chrysostom delivered a sermon on Junia the apostle, who traveled with her husband Andronicus preaching the gospel from city to city, to serve as a paragon for women to emulate. See Bernadette Brooten, "Junia . . . Outstanding among the Apostles," in *Women Priests,* ed. Leonard and Arlene Swidler (New York: Paulist Press, 1977), 141–143.

13. Throughout the New Testament, the Greek word for pastor, *poimēn,* is not used in reference to a woman or a man. What today we call "pastor" was then the person whose house was used as the gathering place for the church. At the homes of these women, the church met, and they served as the church's overseer *(episcopos),* a term evolved to mean "bishop."

14. Karen Jo Torjesen, *When Women Were Priests: Women's Leadership in the Early Church and the Scandal of Their Subordination in the Rise of Christianity* (New York: HarperSanFrancisco, 1995), 2, 6–7, 11, 33.

Bibliography

Every semester when I teach the course *Reading the Bible from the Margins,* I change the books required for the class. This insures a constant flow of new material for the students. The information, ideas, and concepts expressed throughout this book are mostly based on the many scholars who have committed themselves to reading the Bible from the margins. Below is a list of their works, responsible for the formation of the course I teach, of this book, and of my personal reading of the biblical text during my own times of meditation.

Adam, A. K. M., ed. *Handbook of Postmodern Biblical Interpretation.* St. Louis: Chalice Press, 2000.

Amaladoss, Michael. *Life in Freedom: Liberation Theologies from Asia.* Maryknoll: Orbis Books, 1997.

Bailey, Randall C., and Jacquelyn Grant, eds. *The Recovery of the Black Presence: An Interdisciplinary Exploration.* Nashville: Abingdon Press, 1995.

Bañuelas, Arturo, ed. *Mestizo Christianity: Theology from the Latino Perspective.* Maryknoll: Orbis Books, 1995.

Cannon, Katie Geneva. *Katie's Canon: Womanists and the Soul of the Black Community.* New York: Continuum, 1995.

Chung, Hyun Kyung. *Struggle to Be the Sun Again: Introducing Asian Women's Theology.* Maryknoll: Orbis Books, 1991.

Comstock, Gary David. *Gay Theology without Apology.* Cleveland: Pilgrim Press, 1993.

Cone, Cecil. *The Identity Crisis in Black Theology.* Nashville: AMEC, 1975.

Cone, James H. *A Black Theology of Liberation.* 20th Anniversary Edition. Maryknoll: Orbis Books, 1999.

Daly, Mary. *Beyond God the Father: Toward a Philosophy of Women's Liberation.* Boston: Beacon Press, 1973.

De La Torre, Miguel A., and Edwin D. Aponte. *Introducing Latino/a Theologies.* Maryknoll: Orbis Books, 2001.

Douglas, Kelly Brown. *The Black Christ.* Maryknoll: Orbis Books, 1994.

Dussel, Enrique. *Ethics and Community.* Trans. by Robert R. Barr. Maryknoll: Orbis Books, 1988.

Elizondo, Virgilio. *Galilean Journey: The Mexican-American Promise,* rev. ed. Maryknoll: Orbis Books, 2000.

Ellacuría, Ignacio, and Jon Sobrino, eds. *Mysterium Liberationis: Fundamental Concepts of Liberation Theology.* Maryknoll: Orbis Books, 1993.

Felder, Cain Hope, ed. *Stony the Road We Trod: African American Biblical Interpretation.* Minneapolis: Fortress Press, 1991.

Fernandez, Eleazar S., and Fernando F. Segovia. *A Dream Unfinished: Theological Reflections on America from the Margins.* Maryknoll: Orbis Books, 2001.

Freire, Paulo. *Pedagogy of the Oppressed,* rev. ed. Trans. by Myra Bergman Ramos. New York: Continuum, 1994.

González, Justo L. *For the Healing of the Nations: A Book of Revelation in an Age of Cultural Conflict.* Maryknoll: Orbis Books, 1999.

———. *Santa Biblia: The Bible through Hispanic Eyes.* Nashville: Abingdon Press, 1996.

Goss, Robert E., and Mona West, eds. *Take Back the Word: A Queer Reading of the Bible.* Cleveland: Pilgrim Press, 2000.

Gottwald, Norman K., and Richard A. Horsley, eds. *The Bible and Liberation: Political and Social Hermeneutics,* rev. ed. Maryknoll: Orbis Books, 1993.

Gutiérrez, Gustavo. *Las Casas: In Search of the Poor of Jesus Christ.* Trans. by Robert R. Barr. Maryknoll: Orbis Books, 1993.

———. *A Theology of Liberation: History, Politics, and Salvation,* rev. ed. Trans. by Sister Caridad Inda and John Eagleson. Maryknoll: Orbis Books, 1993.

———. *The Power of the Poor in History.* Trans. by Robert R. Barr. Maryknoll: Orbis Books, 1984.

———. *We Drink from Our Own Wells: The Spiritual Journey of a People.* Trans. by Matthew J. O'Connell. Maryknoll: Orbis Books, 1992.

Johnson, Elizabeth A. *She Who Is: The Mystery of God in Feminist Theological Discourse.* New York: Crossroad, 1998.

McNeill, John J. *The Church and the Homosexual.* Boston: Beacon Press, 1993.

Park, Andrew Sung. *Racial Conflict and Healing: An Asian-American Theological Perspective.* Maryknoll: Orbis Books, 1998.

Pedraja, Luis G. *Jesus Is My Uncle: Christology from a Hispanic Perspective.* Nashville: Abington Press, 1999.

Peelman, Achiel. *Christ Is a Native American.* Maryknoll: Orbis Books, 1995.

Pobee, John S., and Bärbel Von Wartenberg-Potter, eds. *New Eyes for Reading: Reading and Theological Reflections by Women from the Third World.* Oak Park, IL: Meyer-Stone Books, 1986.

Raboteau, Albert J. *Slave Religion: The "Invisible Institution" in the Antebellum South.* Oxford: Oxford University Press, 1978.

Rodríguez, José David, and Loida I. Martell-Otero, eds. *Teología en Conjunto: A Collaborative Hispanic Protestant Theology.* Louisville: Westminster John Knox Press, 1997.

Ruether, Rosemary. *Sexism and God-Talk: Toward a Feminist Theology.* Boston: Beacon Press, 1983.

Schüssler Fiorenza, Elisabeth. *But She Said: Feminist Practices of Biblical Interpretation.* Boston: Beacon Press, 1992.

Segundo, Juan Luis. *The Liberation of Theology.* Trans. by John Drury. Maryknoll: Orbis Books, 1976.

Sider, Ronald J. *Rich Christians in an Age of Hunger: Moving from Affluence to Generosity.* 20th Anniversary Edition. Nashville: Word Publishing, 1997.

Song, Choan-Seng. *Tell Us Our Names: Story Theology from an Asian Perspective.* Maryknoll: Orbis Books, 1987.

———. *Third-Eye Theology: Theology in Formation in Asian Settings,* rev. ed. Maryknoll: Orbis Books, 1991.

Sugirtharajah, R. S. *Asian Biblical Hermeneutics and Postcolonialism: Contesting the Interpretations.* Maryknoll: Orbis Books, 1998.

———. *Voices from the Margins: Interpreting the Bible in the Third World,* rev. ed. Maryknoll: Orbis Books, 1995.

Swidler, Arlene, ed. *Homosexuality and World Religions.* Valley Forge: Trinity Press International, 1993.

Thandeka. *Learning to Be White: Money, Race, and God in America.* New York: Continuum, 1999.

Tinker, George E. *Missionary Conquest: The Gospel and Native American Cultural Genocide.* Minneapolis: Fortress Press, 1993.

Torjesen, Karen Jo. *When Women Were Priests: Women's Leadership in the Early Church and the Scandal of Their Subordination in the Rise of Christianity.* New York: HarperSanFrancisco, 1995.

Trible, Phyllis. *God and the Rhetoric of Sexuality.* Philadelphia: Fortress Press, 1978.

———. *Texts of Terror: Literary-Feminist Readings of Biblical Narratives.* Philadelphia: Fortress Press, 1984.

Weems, Renita J. *Just a Sister Away: A Womanist Vision of Women's Relationship in the Bible.* San Diego: LuraMedia, 1988.

Williams, Delores S. *Sisters in the Wilderness: The Challenge of Womanist God-Talk.* Maryknoll: Orbis Books, 1993.

Wilson, Nancy L. *Our Tribe: Queer Folks, God, Jesus, and the Bible.* San Francisco: HarperSanFrancisco, 1995.

General Index

Scripture Index

OLD TESTAMENT

NEW TESTAMENT